VIRGINIA'S HISTORIC RESTAURANTS

and their recipes

JOHN F. BLAIR, *Publisher*
Winston-Salem, North Carolina

VIRGINIA'S HISTORIC RESTAURANTS

and their recipes

by DAWN O'BRIEN

Drawings by Patsy Faires

Revised Edition, 1990

Cover photograph by Bernard Carpenter
Composition by Graphic Composition, Inc.
Manufactured by Donnelley Printing Company

Library of Congress Cataloging in Publication Data on page 207.

ACKNOWLEDGMENTS Everybody knows that Broadway's financial backers are called angels. But what is the name given to those who back you with a part of themselves, give you the kind of help money can't buy? Are they archangels? I don't know. I do know that they are a special breed of human being, and I am indebted to them for their help.

To: The chefs who gave, taught and encouraged—even the one who spanked my hand when I was reaching for the wrong utensil.

To: The restaurateurs who shared their restaurant's heritage and renovation with me.

To: The artist, Patsy Faires, for her beautiful pen and ink renderings of the restaurants.

To: Marty Rawson, once again my gourmet mainstay, for helping me test, retest and correct many recipes. Also to Saxton Powell, Betty Jo Gilley, Becky Newton, Martha Gay Morton and Bev Wachtel for their testing abilities.

To: My daughter, Daintry, for photographing many of the restaurants, as well as driving, typing and collating material for me many times.

To: John and Julia Bize who encouraged and guided me in the right direction.

To: My husband, John, and daughter, Heather, who chose to encourage rather than complain.

To: All my guinea pigs who ate the testing dishes. They have so quadrupled in number that it's impossible to name all of them.

To: Virginia Ingram, Marcia Harmon and Brenda Johnson who are collectively the most intuitive, creative and kind people with whom I've been privileged to share my work.

To: John Fries Blair for believing in the written word—especially mine, and manifesting his belief so enthusiastically.

FOREWORD

This book is dedicated to my mama, Saxton West Powell, who taught me that life must be lived extravagantly. That doesn't necessarily require material goods or money—it does require panache. My mother said, "Don't just do a job well—any fool can do that. Do it with flair!"

It's taking the mundane and making it exciting, or, at the very least, attractive. In a sense, my mother's philosophy is appropriate for this book because it is precisely what the truly great chefs do. They take raw ingredients and create with a delicious flair.

When I first embarked upon writing this series my daughter, Daintry, said, "The worst that could happen is you might learn how to cook." True, in the beginning I wasn't a great cook. Then, through writing *North Carolina's Historic Restaurants and Their Recipes*, I experienced a kind of on-the-road education, learning from chefs whose training grounds included everything from mama's kitchen to the famed culinary institutes of the world.

Over and over I heard them say that formal schooling is important, but that expertise is achieved through apprenticing with great chefs. That is where the real tricks and secrets are learned. Then, because good cooking is an art form, a chef's individual creativity emerges. This is how their fame is achieved.

By the time I was researching Virginia, my culinary ability was much improved. My younger daughter, Heather, no longer winced at the thought of another "fancy do-dah" meal. While working on the other book, there were times when her dad slipped her money for authentic junk food. But with the testing of the Virginia recipes, I've seen a more appreciative attitude.

As with North Carolina, the impetus for researching Virginia was the same. I have a particular affinity for historic settings and want to see them preserved. Maybe it's because of the values I grew up with, I don't know, but it seems to me that we learn best from history.

I am especially grateful to those who are willing to salvage our past, particularly our historic buildings. A division of the Department of Cultural Resources designates certain over-fifty-year-old structures as historically significant if a note-worthy event has occurred there or if the building displays architectural integrity.

I truly honor all who rescue these historic buildings, but I loudly applaud those who convert them into viable opera-tions—in particular, restaurants. This is because I have found that, for the most part, the renovators/restaurateurs who care enough to salvage the structural remnants of our past put the same intricate care into preparing unusually fine food.

And that is my mama's philosophy—going the extra step to set whatever you do apart from what has been done before.

CONTENTS

Foreword   vii

MARTHA WASHINGTON INN   1
Abingdon

SUNNYBROOK INN   5
Roanoke

JOSEPH NICHOLS TAVERN   9
Lynchburg

THE WILLSON-WALKER HOUSE RESTAURANT   13
Lexington

SAM SNEAD'S TAVERN   17
Hot Springs

THE HOMESTEAD   21
Hot Springs

WATERWHEEL RESTAURANT IN   25
THE INN AT GRISTMILL SQUARE
Warm Springs

WARM SPRINGS INN AND RESTAURANT   29
Warm Springs

BUCKHORN INN   33
Churchville

McCORMICK'S PUB & RESTAURANT   37
Staunton

THE WHARF DELI & PUB   41
Staunton

LE SNAIL RESTAURANT   45
Charlottesville

MICHIE TAVERN   49
Charlottesville

MILLER'S   53
Charlottesville

SILVER THATCH INN   57
Charlottesville

THE BOAR'S HEAD INN   61
Charlottesville

THE IVY INN   65
Charlottesville

THE VIRGINIAN   69
Charlottesville

PROSPECT HILL   73
Trevilians

BAVARIAN CHEF   77
Madison

THE CONYERS HOUSE   81
Sperryville

SIXTY-SEVEN WATERLOO   85
Warrenton

THE INN AT LITTLE WASHINGTON   89
Washington

SKY CHALET COUNTRY INN   93
Bayse

EDINBURG MILL RESTAURANT   97
Edinburg

WAYSIDE INN   101
Middletown

THE RED FOX TAVERN   105
Middleburg

KING'S COURT TAVERN   109
Leesburg

LAUREL BRIGADE INN   113
Leesburg

EVANS FARM INN   117
McClean

GADSBY'S TAVERN   121
Alexandria

PORTNER'S   125
Alexandria

MOUNT VERNON INN   129
Mount Vernon

KENMORE INN   133
Fredricksburg

LA PETITE AUBERGE   137
Fredricksburg

OLD MUDD TAVERN   141
Thornburg

HANOVER TAVERN   145
Hanover

FOX HEAD INN   149
Manakin-Sabot

LEMAIRE RESTAURANT   153
Richmond

SAM MILLER'S WAREHOUSE   157
Richmond

THE TOBACCO COMPANY RESTAURANT   161
Richmond

TRAVELLER'S RESTAURANT   165
Richmond

HALF WAY HOUSE   169
Petersburg

CHOWNING'S TAVERN   173
Williamsburg

CHRISTIANA CAMPBELL'S TAVERN   177
Williamsburg

KING'S ARMS TAVERN   181
Williamsburg

THE WILLIAMSBURG INN   185
Williamsburg

SMITHFIELD INN AND TAVERN   189
Smithfield

MILTON WARREN'S ICE HOUSE RESTAURANT   193
Virginia Beach

HILDA CROCKETT'S CHESAPEAKE HOUSE   197
Tangier Island

MARTHA WASHINGTON INN
Abingdon

MARTHA WASHINGTON INN

Driving down Main Street in Abingdon, you feel time has become confused. It should be a horse and buggy, not a car, dropping you at the door of the Martha Washington Inn. Today, the inn appears not a stitch different than it did a hundred and fifty years ago when General Francis Preston built this home for his wife and fifteen children.

During subsequent years, the house has served diverse purposes. During the Civil War it was a hospital for both Confederate and Union armies. I was told that sometimes during a full moon the plaintive strains of a violin can be heard. Old-timers insist that the violinist was a young lady who played to ease the pain of her wounded Confederate lover whom she had hidden in the attic when the Yankees took over the hospital.

The inn is a treasure of tales. Stories include the inn's tenure as a girls' school, which was said to have concentrated more on dining room etiquette than academics. And speaking of the dining room, theirs is named the Cameo Room after the girls' yearbook.

Décor and cuisine perform a successful blend of both centuries. The walls are covered in brown velvet with a parade of crystal chandeliers attached as sconces. Among the odd variety of wooden tables are splashes of large green plants.

Having a late dinner in this classic yet comfortable room, my husband, John, and I chose their Coco Shrimp appetizers. These gigantic shrimp are dipped in coconut, then fried. They could easily be a meal in themselves. If you, like my husband, are a beef lover, then the Carpetbagger is their pièce de résistance. John vows that it is the best filet mignon that has ever entered his mouth. My one bite would second that motion, but it was difficult to tear myself away from their equally prized Crab and Shrimp Norfolk.

If you can squeeze it in, dessert is a good old Southern Raisin Bread Pudding or Cherries Jubilee.

A lighter dining choice would be their Fresh Flounder baked

in champagne and herbs. It is accompanied by a house salad and their Dijon Vinaigrette Dressing.

We were pleased to find that the inn's wine list is as simple or lavish as your pocketbook dictates.

It doesn't matter whether you are stopping for breakfast, lunch or dinner, you must not miss seeing the sterling silver banquet table near the lobby. Appraised for $125,000, the table was accidentally stumbled upon in their basement last year.

Steeped in romantic history, we found the inn's food and atmosphere to be the perpetuation of Southern hospitality as it was originally intended.

Martha Washington Inn is located at 150 West Main Street in Abingdon. Breakfast is served from 7:00 a.m. until 10:00 a.m. daily, with a buffet at breakfast on Sunday. Lunch is served from 11:30 a.m. until 2:00 p.m., and dinner is from 5:00 p.m. until 10:00 p.m., Monday through Saturday, with a Friday and Saturday dinner buffet. Sunday brunch is served from 10:00 a.m. until 2:00 p.m., and dinner is from 5:00 p.m. until 9:00 p.m. For reservations (preferred) call (703) 628-3161.

MARTHA WASHINGTON INN'S FLOUNDER FILLET

4 5- to 8-ounce flounder
  fillets
4 12-inch-by 16-inch pieces
  of brown wrapping paper
1 cup butter, melted
1 teaspoon salt

1 teaspoon pepper
2 teaspoons Old Bay
  Seasoning
8 lemon slices
2 carrots, julienned
2 celery stalks, julienned

Place 4 pieces of paper on counter. Pour ¼ cup melted butter onto each paper's center and spread evenly over paper. Season each paper with ¼ teaspoon salt, ¼ teaspoon pepper, and ½ teaspoon Old Bay Seasoning. Place 2 lemon slices in center of paper and cover with julienned celery and carrot strips. Place fillet upside down on top of carrots and celery. Fold paper together; flatten and crease tightly.

Place on greased cookie sheet in 350-degree oven for 7 to 10 minutes. The paper will puff up when done. Take a sharp knife and, cutting an x from corner to corner, peel back. Serves 4.

MARTHA WASHINGTON INN'S
MARTHA'S DELIGHT

4 8-ounce boneless chicken breasts, unskinned
16 ounces country ham, cooked and julienned

rice (follow package directions)

Bake chicken breasts in oven at 350 degrees for about 15 minutes or until done. Heat julienned ham, put over steamed rice, and top with chicken breasts. Cover with Red Eye Gravy (recipe below). Serves 4.

Red Eye Gravy:
fat scraps from country ham
pepper to taste

1 teaspoon cornstarch
3 to 4 drops of coffee

Take all fat and scraps from ham and place in sauté pan and cook down slowly. Take cooked meat scraps from pan and mince finely; return to pan with rendered fat and simmer for approximately 10 to 15 minutes until mixture turns red. Pepper to taste (salt unnecessary). Add about a teaspoon of cornstarch to thicken and a few drops of coffee for color.

SUNNYBROOK INN
Roanoke

SUNNYBROOK INN

After five years as owners of the Buckhorn Inn near Churchville, Janet and Howard Schlosser moved south in search of "an atmosphere that fit home cooking." They found it at Sunnybrook Farm, a 150-acre dairy farm set in the foothills of the Blue Ridge Mountains near Roanoke.

The Sunnybrook property can be traced back to Abraham Brubaker, a farmer who settled in the Roanoke Valley in the early 1800s. Since then, the deed has passed through several owners. Though most of the original estate has been sold off to developers and encroached upon by I-81 and its exit-ramp industries, one can recapture the feeling of Sunnybrook's rural grandeur by visiting the old homestead, a charming, two-story brick home built in 1919 by the Robert Fox Boxely family. The Schlossers purchased the homestead in 1983 and renovated it staying close to the original architecture, finally opening it as the Sunnybrook Inn.

Entering the inn, visitors are greeted by hardwood elegance from the days before prefabricated construction. Stirred lightly by ceiling fans, the air smells of wood, stovetop potpourri and the warm, rich aroma of Grandmother's country cooking. The Schlossers take great pride in making the inn feel like home. Downstairs, they've converted the sitting rooms and what was once a porch (you can still see the original brick wall and the original ceiling) into spacious, yet cozy, dining rooms.

Janet and Howard feel strongly about using traditional ingredients, a passion that keeps them hunting down local recipes, some of them over a hundred years old. That's why all their breads, pies, cakes and rolls are made daily in their own bakery. But what makes the food decidedly original is Janet's way of adding touches of Pennsylvania Dutch cooking to the traditional Southern style.

Down-home favorites at the Sunnybrook Inn include Chesapeake Bay Oysters, golden Fried Chicken, fresh Mountain Trout, Swiss Steak and Country Ham, all served as single orders or as buffet choices on weekends. Of course, in keeping with the spirit of a Sunday afternoon at Grandmother's house, you'll want to indulge in a warm, freshly baked Apple, Cherry, Peach, Blueberry or Peanut Butter pie. And if you're feeling guilty about the calories, just take an after-dinner stroll around the well-kept grounds and enjoy the view of the Blue Ridge Mountains.

It's the next best thing to going home.

Sunnybrook Inn is located in northeast Roanoke on Plantation Road, just five minutes from I-81. Meals are served Monday through Thursday from 8:00 a.m. until 8:00 p.m.; Friday and Saturday from 8:00 a.m. until 9:00 p.m.; and Sunday from 8:00 a.m. until 6:30 p.m. Groups of 15 to 120 are accommodated in private rooms; reservations are requested for large parties. Call (703) 366-4555.

SUNNYBROOK INN'S HUMMINGBIRD CAKE

3 cups flour
2 cups sugar
1 teaspoon salt
1 teaspoon baking soda
1 teaspoon cinnamon
1 cup oil
3 eggs

8-ounce can crushed
  pineapple, with juice
2 cups chopped ripe
  bananas
1 cup chopped pecans
1 teaspoon vanilla

Sift together flour, sugar, salt, baking soda and cinnamon. Fold in oil and eggs. Stir in pineapple, bananas, pecans and vanilla. Grease and flour 3 9-inch cake pans and fill ⅓ full. Bake at 350 degrees for 20 to 25 minutes.

Cream Cheese Icing:
8 ounces cream cheese
1 stick butter

5½ cups confectioners'
  sugar

Beat together cream cheese, butter and sugar. Spread icing between layers and on top and sides. Yields 1 cake.

SUNNYBROOK INN'S CHRISTMAS
CRANBERRY SALAD

9 ounces strawberry Jell-O
1 package fresh cranberries,
  finely chopped
5 cored apples, finely
  chopped

4 peeled oranges, finely
  chopped
2 8-ounce cans crushed
  pineapple
1 cup sugar

Dissolve Jell-O with hot water according to directions. Add cranberies, apples, oranges and pineapple. Mix in sugar. Chill. Serves 10.

SUNNYBROOK INN'S
THREE-VEGETABLE CASSEROLE

1 large bag frozen broccoli,
  carrot and cauliflower
  mix
1 small onion, chopped
2 tablespoons butter
2 cups grated cheese
1 can cream of mushroom
  soup

2 tablespoons mayonnaise
salt and pepper to taste
3 eggs
crushed soda crackers for
  garnish

Cook frozen vegetables according to directions just until thawed. Drain. Sauté onion in butter. Mix together onion, grated cheese, soup, mayonnaise, salt and pepper and eggs. Add to cooked vegetables. Pour entire mixture into a buttered casserole dish. Top with soda crackers and bake at 325 degrees for 30 minutes or until firm. Serves 6.

JOSEPH NICHOLS TAVERN
Lynchburg

JOSEPH NICHOLS TAVERN

The fact that the 1815 Joseph Nichols Tavern is in healthy operation attests to the supportive community in Lynchburg. When the brick, Federal-style structure, which had become known as the Western Hotel, was slated for the demolition crews in 1975, a committed group of townspeople fought and won the battle to preserve this important page of Lynchburg's history.

During the tavern's early years, it was a thriving ordinary, or inn, and rumor has it that Thomas Jefferson slept here on his way from Monticello to his summer home in Poplar Forest. Then sometime after 1840 it served as one of the many brothels that were particularly popular with out-of-towners in those days.

In subsequent years it saw its ups and downs, turning from brothel to rooming house to private home, and finally to an abandoned haven for transients.

Today, through the unceasing efforts of the Restoration and Housing Corporation, the upstairs has been made into apartments, and the downstairs has become a dinner theater with a growing patronage.

Guests dine in a large room decorated with two colonial blue fireplaces and eat at large, linen-covered, family-style tables on a set menu that changes often. The large table gathering fosters a spirit of camaraderie among guests who perhaps have not met before coming to the tavern.

It's rather hard to pinpoint chef Marianne Rhodes's cuisine, but it has a Southern influence without being what is known as "country cooking." The evening that I visited, the menu offered Southern Peanut Soup, a unique Fruit Salad, Stuffed Cabbage Rolls, Pineapple Muffins and Carrot Cake for dessert. I liked the diversity of the menu and was particularly fond of the Pineapple Muffins. Although licensing does not permit the sale of alcoholic beverages, guests may bring their own bottles of wine.

After dinner, guests move across the foyer to the room that has been converted into a theater. Past productions

10

have ranged from Broadway plays to works by local play-wrights. Recently, a group of players from Ferrum College has provided most of the entertainment. With successful productions like *Bell Boyd: Southern Spy*, the Joseph Nichols Tavern can offer an evening that is both enlivening and delicious.

Joseph Nichols Tavern is located at Madison and Fifth streets in Lynchburg. The tavern is open seasonally on weekends whenever a local production is scheduled. It is also available for private parties. For reservations call (804) 845-6153.

JOSEPH NICHOLS TAVERN'S STUFFED CABBAGE ROLLS

1 large head of cabbage	½ teaspoon thyme
1½ pounds ground chuck	1 teaspoon salt
1 onion, chopped	½ teaspoon pepper
1 garlic clove, finely chopped	½ cup uncooked rice (boil 3 to 5 minutes)

Cut core out of cabbage and pull off outer leaves; wilt remaining cabbage leaves in boiling water about 5 minutes. Shred remaining head of cabbage. Combine all other ingredients. Make 1- to 2-inch balls out of meat mixture and roll each in wilted cabbage leaf. Serves 4 to 6.

Sauce:

1 16-ounce can tomato sauce	1 tablespoon Worcestershire sauce
1 rounded teaspoon brown sugar	1 teaspoon caraway seeds

Mix tomato sauce with brown sugar, Worcestershire sauce and caraway seeds. Line bottom of a greased 13-inch by 9-inch pan with shredded, uncooked cabbage. Place cabbage rolls on top and cover with sauce. Bake in a 350-degree oven for 1½ hours. Serves 4 to 6.

JOSEPH NICHOLS TAVERN'S BLUEBERRY MUFFINS

2 cups plain flour
½ cup sugar
1 teaspoon salt
2 teaspoons baking powder
1 cup milk

1 egg
⅓ cup oil
1 cup blueberries (frozen, fresh or canned)

Mix flour, sugar, salt and baking powder. Combine milk, egg and oil and add to dry ingredients. Fold in drained blueberries. Pour into greased muffin tins. Bake at 400 degrees for 15 to 20 minutes. Yields 12 to 15 muffins.

JOSEPH NICHOLS TAVERN'S SALAD AND DRESSING

Salad:
1 head Boston lettuce
1 grapefruit, sectioned

1 orange, peeled
12 slices pimientos

Place lettuce leaves on four plates and add 3 to 4 sections of grapefruit, 2 orange slices and 3 pimientos to each. Pour dressing over top. Serves 4.

Dressing:
⅓ cup oil
¼ cup white wine vinegar
1 teaspoon oregano
2 teaspoons sugar

1 teaspoon salt
¼ teaspoon pepper
½ teaspoon parsley

Place all ingredients in blender and blend until mixed. Yields ⅔ cup.

THE WILLSON-WALKER
HOUSE RESTAURANT
Lexington

THE WILLSON-WALKER HOUSE RESTAURANT

Whoever coined the term *Southern hospitality* must have visited Lexington, a delightful little town nestled in the Shenandoah Valley. If visitors to town don't know it already, they quickly learn that two of the South's favorite sons—Stonewall Jackson and Robert E. Lee—were associated with Lexington's renowned colleges. Jackson taught at the Virginia Military Institute before gaining his Civil War fame, while Lee became president of Washington College—now Washington and Lee University—immediately after the war.

The Willson-Walker House Restaurant makes its home in one of the many historic buildings in Lexington. The restaurant takes its name from two of the families associated with the property. In 1820, local merchant William Willson constructed the building as a private residence. The structure changed hands several times before Harry Walker converted it to a grocery store in 1911. Following Walker's death, the bottom floor was occupied by a succession of businesses, while the top floor was made into apartments. In 1983, Josephine Griswold, a local resident who received her training as a chef in New York City, purchased the building and restored the facade to its pre-1911 appearance.

Guests at the Willson-Walker House may dine in either of two charming dining rooms or, weather permitting, on the portico overlooking Main Street. The dining rooms are beautifully decorated in green and peach pastels with original artwork and fireplaces with elegantly marbleized mantels.

Each night, the chef prepares a Veal Medallions Special, a Seafood Special and a Lite Choice, among the other tempting entrées. The night I visited, the Seafood Special was Red Snapper stuffed with mushrooms and spinach and baked in parchment. One of my dinner companions selected Grilled Lamb Chops with Mint and Rosemary Wine Jelly, while the other had Pecan-crusted Pork Tenderloin with Ginger Mayonnaise. After sampling each other's entrées, we agreed that everything had been prepared to perfection.

14

If dinner was delicious, dessert was divine. The Willson-Walker House does all its own baking, and the dessert menu includes choices to satisfy anyone's taste. My Raspberry Cordial Creme Pie was out of this world, rivaled only by my companions' Chocolate Silk Pie in an Oreo Cookie Crust and Black Walnut Ganache Tart.

Historic Lexington is an important part of Virginia's heritage. If you're looking for one of the most popular spots in town today, the Willson-Walker House is truly a treat not to be missed.

The Willson-Walker House Restaurant is located at 30 North Main Street in Lexington. Lunch is served from 11:30 a.m. until 2:30 p.m. and dinner from 5:30 p.m. until 9:00 p.m., Tuesday through Saturday. For reservations (recommended) call (703) 463-3020.

WILLSON-WALKER HOUSE'S CHOCOLATE SILK PIE IN AN OREO COOKIE CRUST

Crust:

Oreo cookies, enough to equal 1½ cups ground

3 tablespoons sugar

6 tablespoons melted butter

Remove white filling from cookies. Grind cookies in food processor. Add sugar and butter. Pat into an 8- or 9-inch pie pan. Bake 8 to 10 minutes in a 375-degree oven. Let cool.

Filling:

1 cup unsalted butter, softened

1 cup powdered sugar

4 ounces best-quality unsweetened chocolate, melted and cooled

2 teaspoons vanilla

2 eggs at room temperature

4 tablespoons amaretto liqueur

Cream butter with sugar in mixer. Add chocolate and vanilla and blend for 10 seconds. Add eggs one at a time and blend until very smooth. Add amaretto and mix well. Transfer to shell and chill. Before serving, garnish with whipped cream dusted with cocoa powder. Yields 1 pie.

15

WILLSON-WALKER HOUSE'S PECAN-CRUSTED PORK TENDERLOIN WITH GINGER MAYONNAISE

Pecan-crusted Pork:

dry breadcrumbs
ground toasted pecans
1½ pounds pork
   tenderloin, sliced

eggs, beaten
4 tablespoons clarified
   butter

Mix breadcrumbs and pecans ½ to ½ and season to taste with salt and pepper. Dip pork slices in eggs, then in crumbs. Sauté in clarified butter. Remove to warm platter.

Ginger Mayonnaise:

1-inch piece fresh ginger,
   peeled
large clove garlic
2 egg yolks at room
   temperature
4 teaspoons white wine
   vinegar
¼ teaspoon salt

¾ cup plus 2½ tablespoons
   vegetable oil
1½ tablespoons sesame oil
4 drops Tabasco sauce
¼ tube sun-dried tomato
   paste
1 green onion, chopped

Mince ginger and garlic in food processor. Add egg yolks, vinegar and salt and blend until smooth. With machine running, add vegetable oil and sesame oil through feed tube until mixture thickens. Add Tabasco and tomato paste. Transfer to a container and stir in onion. To serve, top each slice of pork with mixture. Serves 4.

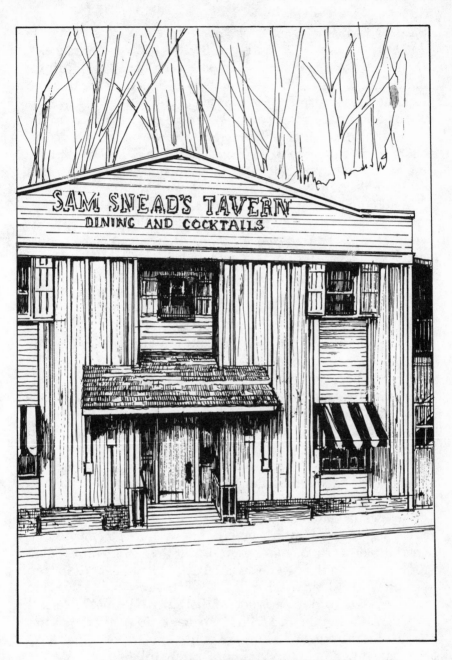

SAM SNEAD'S TAVERN
Hot Springs

SAM SNEAD'S TAVERN

This sporty tavern is definitely a "letting-go" type of place. A few years ago, Hot Springs' famous son, professional golfer Sam Snead, took this old bank and transformed it into a casual club. If you know little about golf before dropping into Sam's, you won't leave in the same condition. Not only did Mrs. Snead make the downstairs into a museum of Sam's vast accomplishments, but the menu, in golf lingo, explains Sam's history, along with that of the building.

When the building was constructed in 1920, it cost $15,000, and the massive vault that you see standing wide open as you enter was purchased for $7,000. The vault, which now holds the tavern's wine, is considered an engineering marvel. The door alone weighs 2,000 pounds, but is balanced so that it can be closed with one hand. The door locks are set by a timing mechanism to open at a specific time only. I'm told that in an emergency, the only alternative would be to blow open the doors, which would, consequently, blow open the building. So far, nobody has needed a bottle of wine that badly.

Maybe it's because the tavern offers such an enticing variety of mixed drinks—everything from a Buzz Bomb to a Piña Colada with vanilla ice cream. I favor the latter, which is served to children minus the rum.

For lunch, I went for the Mexiskins. Hot, hot, and hot, so I cooled the recipe down a tad for you. My main course was their Hickory Smoked Ribs, which, yes, are definitely in the finger lickin' category.

If you are thinking of something not quite so spicy or calorically powerful, you might want their Sunshine Salad topped with sunflower seeds. At dinner, you couldn't go wrong with Allegheny Trout. Just ask them to broil it in wine for you. After dinner, try one of their international coffees.

The restaurant has a Mobil three-star rating, and the promise of their motto, ". . . where you can bank on great food and cocktails," is, in my opinion, amply fulfilled.

Sam Snead's Tavern is located at 1 Main Street in Hot Springs. Meals are served daily from 11:30 a.m. until 9:30 p.m. For reservations (recommended) call (703) 839-2828.

SAM SNEAD'S TAVERN'S HOUSE DRESSING

6 tablespoons honey
¾ cup cider vinegar
1½ cups salad oil
¼ small onion, minced
1 tablespoon parsley

1 tablespoon celery seeds
1 tablespoon poppy seeds
½ tablespoon ground
mustard
½ teaspoon paprika

Put all ingredients in blender and blend on high speed until creamy. Yields about 3 cups.

SAM SNEAD'S TAVERN'S MEXISKINS

2 large baked potatoes
4 ounces hamburger
2 tablespoons onions, diced
2 tablespoons green
peppers, diced
1 tablespoon jalapeño
peppers, diced

2 tablespoons tomatoes,
chopped
2 teaspoons chili powder
3 ounces Cheddar cheese,
shredded
3 ounces Monterey Jack,
shredded

Slice potatoes in quarters and scoop out to ¼ inch from skin. Cook hamburger until pink disappears. Add diced onions, both varieties of peppers and chopped tomatoes, sautéing until translucent. Add chili powder, mixing well. Fill skins with mixture and top evenly with shredded cheeses. Place under broiler until cheese melts. Serves 2.

SAM SNEAD'S TAVERN'S PIÑA COLADA

2½ cups chunk pineapple
  and juice
½ cup creme of coconut

2 heavy pinches shredded
  coconut

Blend pineapple, creme of coconut and shredded coconut in blender. Mix is enough for 12 servings.

¼ cup blended mix
1½ ounces light rum
1 scoop vanilla ice cream
1½ scoops ice

½ teaspoon shredded
  coconut
1 cherry

Place ¼ cup of prepared pineapple mix in blender and add rum, ice cream and ice. Blend until frothy. Pour into glass and top with shredded coconut and a cherry. Serves 1.

THE HOMESTEAD
Hot Springs

THE HOMESTEAD In the early 1900s you were ad-
mitted to The Homestead only if
society had recorded your name
in its Blue Book. The story goes that two dowagers were
rocking on the veranda, and one of them said, "Those people
coming up the walk aren't in the Book. Why would The
Homestead admit them?"

"Maybe The Homestead needs the money," replied the
other.

"Well, *really*, couldn't they just send the money, I mean,
must they come?"

Ah, yes, why spoil life for the aristocracy? They had been
coming to partake of the curative hot springs and mountain
air since 1766 when the first inn was built. Nevertheless, after
Pearl Harbor, the State Department chose The Homestead as
the ideal place of internment for the Japanese diplomatic
staff. Since geography virtually cloisters the inn in a crevice
of the Allegheny Mountains, the staff was protected in luxury for the first months of the war.

Although war and changing social mores did disturb this
playground for the "Blue Bookers," old world manners still
remain. For the first time in my tour of restaurants, I saw a
maître d' slide a silver crumber over the white linen tablecloth to collect the luncheon crumbs before dessert was served.
I was so fascinated watching the crumber glide around the
fresh bouquet of tulips that I spilled my hot tea. So much for
my admittance to Blue Book society.

Seriously, though, my Southern lunch of Short Ribs, deli-
cately cooked with a light sauce, was really very good, and I
especially enjoyed their preparation of zucchini. I found the
Raspberry Poppy Seed Dressing to be so exceptional that I
went back into their cavernous kitchen to get the recipe for
you. I also toured the pastry kitchen, snacking all the way
down into the wine cellar, which has a selection to please
any royal taste.

There are many dining rooms in this majestic Kentucky-
brick, five-star resort, but I felt fortunate to lunch in the

Dining Room. Its dance floor is partitioned with Corinthian columns, giving the room an atrium effect. The Homestead has been called a social spa, Versailles and a palace. To me it was a castle with an underground moat of bubbling hot springs, where I had a wonderful time.

The Homestead is located on Route 220 in Hot Springs. In the Dining Room, breakfast is served from 7:30 a.m. until 9:30 a.m., and dinner is served from 7:00 p.m. until 8:30 p.m. In the Grille Room, breakfast is served from 7:00 a.m. until 9:00 a.m.; lunch is served from noon until 2:00 p.m.; dinner is served from 7:00 p.m. until 10:00 p.m.; and supper is served from 10:00 p.m. until midnight. Service in the Grille Room is seasonal. In the Casino, a luncheon buffet is served daily in season from noon until 2:30 p.m. For reservations (recommended) call (703) 839-5500.

THE HOMESTEAD'S RASPBERRY
POPPY SEED DRESSING

1½ cups sugar	2 tablespoons onion juice
⅔ cup raspberry vinegar	2 cups vegetable oil
1 teaspoon English mustard	3 tablespoons poppy seeds
1 teaspoon salt	

Mix everything together in a blender except oil and poppy seeds. Blend well. Add oil slowly until dressing reaches thick consistency. Add poppy seeds and blend. Serve over salad. Yields 1 quart.

THE HOMESTEAD'S CREAM OF WATERCRESS

1 bunch of watercress	¼ stalk of celery, sliced
6 tablespoons butter	1 small leek, diced
4 tablespoons chicken stock	1½ ounces flour
1 small onion, chopped	1 cup half and half

Pick the leaves from a large bunch of watercress. Chop leaves and simmer in 2 tablespoons butter and 2 tablespoons chicken stock for 5 minutes and set aside. Cut up coarsely the stems of the remaining watercress and mix with onion, celery and leek. Simmer in 2 tablespoons of butter and 2 tablespoons chicken stock for 30 minutes. Stir into a combined mixture of 2 tablespoons melted butter and 1½ ounces flour. Bring to a boil. Add half and half, stirring constantly, and simmer for 10 minutes. Strain. Add the precooked watercress leaves to the liquid. Season to taste with salt. If too thick, add more cream or milk. Serve hot. Serves 4.

THE HOMESTEAD'S ROAST TURKEY "MARCO POLO"

2 bunches fresh broccoli **Mornay Sauce**
12 slices roasted turkey **Parmesan cheese to taste**

Boil broccoli until barely tender. Place broccoli in greased casserole dish and cover with sliced, hot turkey so that only tops of broccoli show. Cover completely with Mornay Sauce (recipe below). Sprinkle Parmesan cheese on top and place under broiler until golden brown. Serves 4.

Mornay Sauce:
3 tablespoons butter **salt to taste**
2 tablespoons flour **white pepper to taste**
2 cups milk, heated **¼ cup ham, julienned**
¼ cup grated Parmesan **¼ cup mushrooms,**
** cheese** ** julienned**

Melt butter in pan, add flour to make roux. Set aside to cool for 2 to 3 minutes. Add hot milk, stir until boiling, then simmer for 5 to 10 minutes. (Add more milk to thin if necessary.) Add cheese, salt, pepper, ham and mushrooms. Simmer until cheese melts and mushrooms are heated.

WATERWHEEL RESTAURANT
THE INN AT GRISTMILL SQUARE
Warm Springs

WATERWHEEL RESTAURANT

Nestled in the valley of the Allegheny Mountains is the Inn at Gristmill Square. My first impression was "I know that painting" because the setting looks like a nineteenth century work of art in the Hudson River genre. Modern cars and telephone wires reminded me that I hadn't slipped into a time warp.

The large, twenty-foot waterwheel on the side of the red wooden restaurant was once powered by a ninety-eight-degree creek heated from the igneous rocks of the famous warm springs. The wheel can still turn just as it did back in 1771 when miller Jacob Butler ground his cornmeal for spoonbread and hoe cakes. Today, at the converted Waterwheel Restaurant, your palate will experience far more sophisticated fare.

Inside, the restaurant's décor has an inviting, posh, country look. The wide plank walls have been whitewashed and hold candle lanterns which cast a soft, unobtrusive light.

Before dining, you can go into the gravel-floored wine cellar and select from wines displayed amidst the mechanism that once powered the waterwheel. Back upstairs, some of the mill's original tools, such as grinding presses, continue to stand where they were installed. Because you are in an old mill, the equipment does not seem out of place with tables set with pink linen tablecloths, fresh flowers and wine-colored china.

I had been overindulging so I chose their Trout broiled in garlic and wine. Before the entrée, a relish tray of Marinated Vegetables was served. This course was followed by a fresh green salad accompanied by a small loaf of freshly baked bread on its own cutting board. The Trout dish was decidedly one of the best I've ever tasted. If, however, you don't need to cut calories, your interest might lie in an appetizer of Seviche followed by Honey Mustard Glazed Spareribs, Chicken Tarragon or a French preparation of Duck.

For dessert I tried one bite of their Apple Cake with Rum Sauce and one bite of their Chocolate Mousse. After dinner I visited their quaint pub, named after the heroic pioneer

Simon Kenton. I had a marvelous liqueur-embellished coffee and thought that if I had been the rating party from Mobil, this restaurant and charming inn would have netted five stars instead of four.

The Waterwheel Restaurant in the Inn at Gristmill Square is located in Warm Springs. Its menu changes at least every six months. Lunch is served from noon until 2:00 p.m. Friday and Saturday. Dinner is served from 6:00 p.m. until 9:00 p.m., Tuesday through Thursday, and from 6:00 p.m. until 10:00 p.m., Friday and Saturday. Sunday brunch is served from 11:00 a.m. until 2:00 p.m. For reservations (recommended) call (703) 839-2231.

WATERWHEEL RESTAURANT'S SCALLOP SEVICHE A LA TALLITIENNE

1½ pounds fresh scallops
2 tablespoons olive oil
1 teaspoon salt
3 tablespoons chopped
  parsley
½ cup strained lime juice
⅛ teaspoon minced garlic
1 tablespoon freshly
  crushed black
  peppercorns

Combine all ingredients in a shallow ceramic or glass bowl and chill, covered, for 3 hours (or overnight). Stir occasionally. Serve in a small cocktail glass or a small, carved out pineapple. Serves 4.

WATERWHEEL RESTAURANT'S HONEY MUSTARD GLAZED SPARERIBS

2 cups orange juice
¼ cup soy sauce
3 garlic cloves, crushed
¼ teaspoon ginger (fresh or ground)
¼ cup grated orange peel
1 cup pure honey
3 teaspoons hot mustard (or Dijon-style)
16 pork spareribs, boiled until tender
rice (follow package directions)
chopped parsley

Mix all ingredients well except rice and spareribs. Pour mixture over ribs and cover with foil. Marinate overnight. The next day, broil ribs in same juice until crisp and let set in warm oven (375 degrees) for 15 minutes. Serve with rice sprinkled with chopped parsley. Serves 4.

WATERWHEEL RESTAURANT'S CHICKEN IN TARRAGON CREAM SAUCE

whole chicken, skinned, cut up and lightly floured
¼ cup butter
¼ cup oil
4 large shallots, peeled and finely chopped
½ cup white wine
2 cups chicken stock
¼ cup fresh cream
¼ cup chives, chopped
1½ cups fresh mushrooms, sliced
¼ cup brandy
½ teaspoon tarragon (fresh or dried)
¼ cup fresh parsley, finely chopped
salt and pepper to taste
rice or potatoes

Sauté chicken parts in ¼ cup soft butter plus ¼ cup of oil until golden. Put aside. Sauté shallots in the same pan and stir with wooden spoon until light yellow. Glaze with white wine; add chicken stock. Reduce heat. Add cream, chives and mushrooms and stir. Add chicken parts to sauce; cook over low flame for 15 minutes. Add brandy, tarragon, parsley, salt and pepper. Cook 5 more minutes. Serve with rice or parsleyed potatoes. Serves 4.

WARM SPRINGS INN AND RESTAURANT
Warm Springs

WARM SPRINGS INN AND RESTAURANT

Nothing, but nothing, smells more inviting than apple butter cooking in an uncovered crock pot. The early spring morning that I breakfasted at Warm Springs, that aroma tinged the air.

The dining room tables and windows at the Warm Springs Inn are full of potted flowers grown by Grandmother Routier, wife of the late Edmund Routier, who first came to America as pastry chef for The Homestead. The Routiers' granddaughter, Michelle, told me that more than forty years ago, her grandparents converted a 1791 jail and courthouse into this inn and restaurant.

The lobby, which once served as the courthouse, is decorated with white wicker settees comfortably arranged around the fireplace. There is no designer touch to the room. It is simply a reflection of the family's interests. Perhaps the most remarkable items in the lobby are Chef Routier's paintings, which were done in the medium of bakers' cocoa. The paintings of Winston Churchill and friends resemble softly etched pastels, but one that had a more abstract quality seems to have suffered from its proximity to the fireplace, which caused the cocoa to melt. Apparently, to cook with cocoa and have those culinary masterpieces consumed is a compliment, but it is a different story when the function of the masterpiece is to hang on the wall.

The current generation of Routiers does not, however, consider its foods to be masterpieces, just simple mountain fare with French overtones. They make all of their own jams and jellies. The most popular is their Peach Butter, with close competition from Apple Butter, Raspberry Jam, Strawberry Jam, Peach Jelly and Grape Jelly.

Interest in the "therapeutic" baths that were so popular in the nineteenth century has been revitalized recently. Whether the baths are in or out of fashion, people continue to return every season for the warm hospitality and food at this charming old bed-and-breakfast inn snuggled in the lap of the Allegheny Mountains.

Warm Springs Inn and Restaurant is located in Warm Springs at Highways 220 and 39. Breakfast is served from 7:00 a.m. until 10:00 a.m. For reservations (preferred) call (703) 839-5351.

WARM SPRINGS INN'S PEACH BUTTER

peaches to yield 2 quarts of   4 sterilized pint jars
   pulp
4 cups sugar

Scald, peel, pit and chop peaches. Place peaches into a 5-quart Dutch oven or large pot. Over medium heat, cook until soft, adding only enough water to prevent sticking. Remove peaches and press through a sieve or a food mill. Measure 2 quarts of pulp. Return pulp to pot and add sugar. Cook on medium-low heat for about 30 minutes. As mixture thickens, stir frequently to prevent sticking. Pour mixture into newly sterilized, hot jars. Leave 1/4 inch of space at top. Screw on caps over lids and place jars in sterilizing pot. Cover with hot water and boil for 10 minutes. Remove and tighten caps. Yields 4 pints.

WARM SPRINGS INN'S CHEESE OMELET

2 strips bacon   salt and pepper to taste
2 teaspoons butter   4 tablespoons sharp
2 eggs   cheddar cheese, shredded
2 tablespoons milk   1 teaspoon tomato, diced

Fry bacon in a skillet; cool, crumble and set aside. Melt butter in an omelet pan. Mix eggs with milk, salt and pepper and add to pan. Gently scramble the eggs until they begin to set. Add cheese, tomato and bacon to center of eggs and fold eggs in half. Serve on a warm plate. Serves 1.

WARM SPRINGS INN'S
CROCK POT APPLE BUTTER

12 to 14 cooking apples
2 cups apple juice
2½ cups sugar
1½ teaspoons cinnamon

½ teaspoon cloves
5 or more sterilized ½-pint jars

Wash, core and quarter apples, but do not peel them. Fill lightly oiled crock pot with apples and apple juice. Cover and cook on low for 2 to 4 hours, until apples are tender. Remove apple mixture and press through sieve or food mill. Measure apple mixture and return to crock pot. Add 1 cup sugar per pint of apples. Add cinnamon and cloves. Cover and cook on high for 6 to 8 hours, stirring every 2 hours. Remove cover after 3 hours to allow mixture to cook down. Pour mixture into newly sterilized, hot jars. Screw on caps over lids and place in boiling water for 10 minutes. Remove and tighten caps. Yields 5 or more ½-pint jars.

BUCKHORN INN
Churchville

BUCKHORN INN

From the Buckhorn Inn's upstairs veranda, which encircles the inn, the distant view of the Shenandoah Mountains became the most soothing moment of my day. Pastel blossoming dogwoods and lilacs polka-dotting the dusky landscape resembled the country quilt on my bed in the antique-appointed bedroom.

Feeling more at peace after my veranda visit, I descended the curving staircase that Stonewall Jackson and his wife Elinor had trod back in 1854 when they stayed at this inn. It seems that from 1800 to 1861 the Buckhorn Tavern, as it was then known, was a popular stop for stagecoaches carrying folks, such as the Jacksons, who were on their way to the famed hot springs in Bath County.

Later, when the Civil War engulfed this serene territory, the Buckhorn became a hospital for the soldiers who were wounded during the Battle of McDowell. With the many changes that followed the war, the tavern became a dance hall and gambling house where it is believed a gambler was either murdered or committed suicide in what is now a passageway to the kitchen. The Buckhorn employees told me they occasionally experience the presence of the dead man's spirit in a variety of unexplained ways.

Hanging around to help food disappear as it emerges from the kitchen is probably one of the spirit's more vexing manifestations. I don't blame him, though, because the bountiful array of country-style food poses a definite temptation. Many of the recipes are from the Shenandoah Valley and have been handed down for generations.

I dined in a pre-Civil War room that was original to the house. I'm told that the room's beautiful pine walls were stripped of uncountable coats of paint during renovation. It was worth the effort as the wood adds a warm, rich feel to the room.

I enjoyed a tender and juicy London Broil for dinner with Mashed Potatoes, Broccoli Salad, Marinated Carrots and Spiced Fruits. That doesn't sound like typical country cooking, but it is of this region. I particularly liked the Broccoli Salad. I would also recommend the Fried Chicken or Oysters, and the Peanut Butter Pie was superb.

The Buckhorn stocks a good variety of domestic wines, particularly from the Shenandoah Vineyards. I didn't sample the wine as the atmosphere of the Buckhorn had already produced a mellowing effect that I didn't want to alter.

The Buckhorn Inn is located on Route 250 near Churchville, twelve miles west of Staunton. Family-style meals are served from 11:00 a.m. until 5:00 p.m., Tuesday through Thursday, and from 11:00 a.m. until 4:00 p.m. on Friday. Buffets are served from 5:00 p.m. until 8:00 p.m., Tuesday through Thursday, and from 4:00 p.m. until 9:00 p.m. on Friday and Saturday. The Sunday buffet is served from 11:00 a.m. until 8:00 p.m. No reservations are accepted, but if you need to call the inn for lodging, the phone number is (703) 337-6900.

BUCKHORN INN'S BROCCOLI SALAD

1 bunch broccoli, chopped
¼ cup onions, chopped
¼ cup green olives,
  chopped

4 eggs, boiled and chopped
½ cup sugar
1 cup mayonnaise

In a one-quart bowl, mix all ingredients together until mixture is well blended. Refrigerate. Serves 10 to 12.

BUCKHORN INN'S MARINATED CARROTS

5 cups sliced carrots
1 medium onion
1 small green pepper
1 10½-ounce can of cream of tomato soup
½ cup salad oil
1 cup sugar

¾ cup cider vinegar
1 teaspoon prepared mustard
1 teaspoon Worcestershire sauce
1 teaspoon salt
½ teaspoon pepper

Put carrots in water and bring to a boil. Reduce heat to medium and cook until tender. Drain and cool. Cut onion and green pepper in round slices and mix with cooled carrots. Mix all other ingredients together in separate container and pour over vegetables. Cover and marinate in refrigerator for at least 12 hours. Drain to serve. Will keep for 2 weeks in refrigerator. Serves 8 to 10.

BUCKHORN INN'S PEANUT BUTTER PIE

⅓ cup creamy peanut butter
¾ cup confectioners' sugar

1 9-inch pie shell, baked

Mix peanut butter and sugar together until crumbly and place on bottom of crust, saving 2 tablespoons to sprinkle on top.

Filling:
⅓ cup flour
½ cup sugar
⅛ teaspoon salt
2 cups milk
2 egg yolks (slightly beaten)

2 teaspoons margarine, melted
1 teaspoon vanilla
prepared whipped topping

Mix first five ingredients together in a saucepan over high heat until mixture comes to a rolling boil. Stir until mixture reaches thick consistency. Remove filling from heat and add melted margarine and vanilla.

Pour over peanut butter mixture and cool. Spread with prepared whipped topping. Sprinkle with leftover peanut butter crumbles. Refrigerate. Yields 1 pie.

McCORMICK'S PUB & RESTAURANT
Staunton

McCORMICK'S PUB & RESTAURANT

It is impossible to put a price on time, but when there is little, it becomes precious. Because Staunton's downtown business people have limited time for lunch, McCormick's prides itself on serving patrons quickly and in plenty of time to return to the office.

The day I lunched in this tastefully decorated establishment, accented by green grasscloth walls and gold linen tablecloths, they were ready with an excellent Cabbage Soup containing garbanzo beans, chunks of sausage and bacon. This was *quickly* followed by a yummy Broccoli Cheddar Quiche with a hefty helping of authentic German Potato Salad and crisp Cole Slaw.

Dieters can always have a choice of slenderizing salads, but you might not want to diet, especially since that would mean giving up their famed Irish Whiskey Pie, which, thankfully, I did not. I didn't even go to their spa afterward to work off those extra calories, another option when dining at this restaurant.

McCormick's has access to a spa because it was originally a YMCA back in 1915. It seems that Staunton wanted a Y but could not come up with the necessary funds until someone got the idea to approach the Cyrus Hall McCormick family. The renowned farm machinery family offered to match whatever funds the city could raise. This innovative approach to philanthropy became the forerunner to the current method of matching grants.

At any rate, a sizable amount must have been raised as the interior is grand. You will be impressed with the handsome marble entrance leading to the former lobby, which now serves as a pub.

The lobby is paneled in walnut cut at the McCormick estate. This wood was used lavishly by skilled valley craftsmen to create everything from the mantle pieces to a wonderful, curving bar. Still ticking in the lobby after almost seven decades is a Seth Thomas clock, now valued at $10,000.

This luxuriously serene lobby is a great place to enjoy happy hour, particularly after a hectic day at work.

Dinner offers such gourmet specialties as the Fillet of Beef McCormick or the McCormick Reaper, which is roast beef and Brie on a croissant and accompanied by a stuffed potato.

Of course any of their luncheon or dinner meals may be complemented with a selection of imported wines and beers to afford you a pleasant experience at the old Y.

McCormick's Pub & Restaurant is located at 41 North Augusta Street in Staunton. Meals are served from 11:30 a.m. until midnight, Monday through Friday and from 11:30 a.m. until 1:00 a.m. on Saturday. For reservations (preferred) call (703) 885-3111.

McCORMICK'S JAMBALAYA

1 teaspoon vegetable oil
1 teaspoon cayenne pepper
½ teaspoon paprika
¼ teaspoon thyme
8 ounces medium shrimp, cleaned and deveined
2 strips uncooked bacon, chopped
½ medium green pepper, chopped
2 scallions, chopped
1 medium boiled potato, peeled and chopped
1 cup canned tomatoes, chopped
4 ounces tomato paste
2 lemon wedges
salt and pepper to taste
1 cup cooked rice

Place oil in skillet over medium heat and add cayenne pepper, paprika and thyme, stirring to combine. Stir in shrimp and cook for 1 minute. Add bacon, green pepper and scallions and cook for 4 minutes. Add potato, tomatoes and tomato paste, stirring to incorporate, and let simmer until cooked. Squeeze juice of lemon into mixture and add rind. Season with salt and pepper. Mix and serve over rice. Serves 2.

McCORMICK'S TOFFEE SHORTBREAD

Crust:

1¼ cups all-purpose flour   ½ cup melted butter
¼ cup sugar

In a medium-sized bowl, combine ingredients and mix until texture is crumbly. Grease a 10-inch flan pan or a pan of equivalent size and press mixture into pan. Bake in a pre-heated 350-degree oven for 15 minutes.

Filling:

¾ cup butter   1 tablespoon light corn
¾ cup sweetened   syrup
** condensed milk   1 teaspoon vanilla**
½ cup sugar

In a small saucepan, melt the butter over low heat and add remaining ingredients. Raise heat and bring to a boil. Stir constantly for 4 minutes. Pour into crust and let cool.

Topping:

1 tablespoon butter   2 squares semisweet
**   chocolate**

Melt butter and chocolate together and pour over pie. Let cool and cut into squares. Yields 9 or more squares.

THE WHARF DELI & PUB
Staunton

THE WHARF DELI & PUB

I always thought the word "wharf" referred to the waterfront, so when there was no body of water anywhere near the Wharf Deli & Pub, I was confused. Then I discovered the Old English word "wharf" has another denotation. Wharf can also mean warehouse, which is what this restaurant, built as a grocery store in 1880, eventually became.

This interestingly mismatched brick building has passed from grocery store to veterinarian's hospital, and was last used as a garage and auto parts warehouse.

When the renovators began redesigning the building, they rescued a tremendous skylight from an old bank building slated for demolition. Installing the skylight into the second-floor roof opened the dark corners with a flood of sunlight and dramatically transformed the upstairs into a spacious room resembling an artist's loft. Large trees, planted in tubs, receive the necessary sunshine, and some leftover tin Coca Cola, Pepsi and Wolf's Head Oil signs are hung on the textured brick walls to strike a nostalgic chord from the past.

Sitting on an old wooden bench, I listened to the music drift upstairs. As a New York deli devotee, I was ecstatic to find the real thing in such pleasant surroundings, as delis are not known for especially attractive décor.

Whereas the house wine is usually a good barometer for formal restaurants, at a deli it's the chicken salad, slaw and potato salad that give the important clues. I check the usual meats and cheeses, but if a deli scores on their homemade items, then chances look good for the others. Verdict: The Chicken Salad was very good with nice chunks of chicken in a savory mixture, and the spicy, red cabbage Slaw was perfect with a Coors beer. (You might want to try one of their other forty-nine imported beers.) Best of all was dessert. I took more than one bite of their rich German Chocolate Pie because it was so scrumptious.

You'd think that dieting would be difficult, but they do offer a low-cal Cottage Cheese Plate with assorted cheeses for times when heavier selections are verboten.

The Wharf Deli & Pub is located at 123 South Augusta Street in Staunton. Meals are served from 11:00 a.m. until 3:00 p.m. on Monday, from 11:00 a.m. until 9:00 p.m. on Tuesday through Thursday, and from 11:00 a.m. until 10:00 p.m. on Friday and Saturday. For reservations (preferred for large parties) call (703) 886-2329.

THE WHARF DELI'S CHICKEN SALAD

1 chicken, cooked and cut
   into bite-size pieces
1 medium onion, chopped
2 large celery stalks,
   chopped

1 teaspoon white pepper
1 teaspoon salt
1 teaspoon celery seeds
¾ cup mayonnaise

After chicken has been cut into bite-size pieces, place in a bowl. Add chopped onion and chopped celery. Season with white pepper, salt and celery seeds. Spoon in mayonnaise and mix until all ingredients are thoroughly combined. Chill, covered in refrigerator. Serves 6 to 8.

THE WHARF DELI'S GERMAN CHOCOLATE PIE

4 ounces unsweetened
   chocolate
¼ cup butter
1 cup sugar
1 14-ounce can sweetened
   condensed milk

3 egg yolks
1 cup shredded coconut
1 unbaked pie shell

Place chocolate and butter in a small saucepan over medium heat until melted, stirring constantly. Remove and pour chocolate mixture into bowl. Add sugar, beat with electric mixer. Stir in milk, mixing thoroughly. Add egg yolks, one at a time, beating until well incorporated. Add coconut. Allow chocolate mixture to cool, then pour into pie shell and bake at 350 degrees for 45 to 50 minutes. Cool and serve. Yields 1 pie.

THE WHARF DELI'S
BROCCOLI AND CHEESE SOUP

1 cup margarine
flour
1 quart instant non-fat
  dried milk, mixed
4 cups chicken broth or
  stock
1 cup chopped broccoli

1 cup Cheddar cheese,
  shredded
1 scant teaspoon white
  pepper
1 scant teaspoon garlic
  powder
2 tablespoons chicken base

Melt margarine over medium heat in a large pot. Add flour a little at a time, stirring into a roux. Add instant milk and chicken broth, stirring with a whisk. After mixture begins to thicken, add broccoli and cheese, and then pepper, garlic powder and chicken base to taste. Yields ½ gallon.

LE SNAIL RESTAURANT
Charlottesville

LE SNAIL
RESTAURANT

If escargot is on the menu, you may be sure it will be my first choice, and dining at Le Snail, that seemed the most appropriate choice. The Austrian-trained chef and owner, Ferdinand Bazin, has given this appetizer a creative touch by nesting the escargot in puff pastry.

I began my sampling sitting on an old church pew in the bar, then moved into a beautiful back dining room where the walls had been painstakingly hand-stenciled by Bazin's wife, Judy. This type of stenciling, a French method too difficult to explain, creates an air of chic elegance.

Originally, Le Snail was a private residence. Built between 1880 and 1890, it later served as the home and office of the first black physician to graduate from the University of Virginia. That gentleman was Dr. Marshall T. Garrett, who did more for his community than minister to its ill health. In addition to his practice, Garrett became known as a community leader responsible for bringing about the reform of health care for prisoners.

It has been said that there are no accidents—fate directs our moves. Bazin believes Le Snail is housed in this quaint old home because of his own need for a physical examination. His first visit to the residence was as a patient, but his return was as master chef and proprietor.

Bazin puts special time and effort into creating his basically French cuisine. Another of my appetizer samplings was Smoked Salmon on freshly baked French bread with a dollop of Ravigot dressing. It was delicate and delicious, as was their Pâté made without preservatives. That evening I was having an appetizer feast, so I went on to sample their unique Bluefish. The fish is smoked and marinated to give it a distinct but delightful flavor.

Like most Americans, I grew up on *Peter Cottontail*, so it was difficult for me to even think of sampling the Lapin. But to my surprise, it was excellent! Bazin thinks rabbit will become the chicken of tomorrow. He could be right.

I bowed out of dessert but would recommend the Crepe Maison flambéed tableside. It looked most appealing.

The Bazins were labeled "brave pioneers" when they restored their restaurant, and their courage and artistry have created a success.

Le Snail is located at 320 West Main Street in Charlottesville. Dinner is served Monday through Saturday from 6:00 p.m. until 10:00 p.m. The restaurant is closed the last week of December, the first two weeks in January and three weeks in August. For reservations (recommended) call (804) 295-4456.

LE SNAIL'S CRAB AU FOUR

1 pound crabmeat, drained
1 tablespoon salt
½ tablespoon pepper
½ tablespoon chopped
  garlic clove
2 tablespoons
  Worcestershire sauce
1 lemon rind, grated
3 teaspoons parsley,
  chopped
¼ cup white wine

½ cup sliced mushrooms
2 tablespoons hazelnuts,
  chopped
½ cup onions, chopped
1 cup sour cream
juice of 1 lemon
¼ cup bread crumbs, fine
Hollandaise sauce (use
  prepared mix or your
  favorite recipe)
optional garnish

Combine all ingredients except Hollandaise in bowl and mix thoroughly. Let set for thirty minutes. Spoon into 12 individual oven-proof dishes or large casserole dish. Cover with Hollandaise and bake at 350 degrees for 15 minutes. Garnish with lemon slices, tomatoes, cucumbers and sprigs of parsley if desired. Serves 12 appetizers or 6 entrées.

LE SNAIL'S FILLET LAPIN

2 2- to 3-pound rabbits or
   fillets
4 slices bacon
pinch of salt, pepper,
   paprika and thyme

flour to dust
1 tablespoon oil
1 apple, sliced
prepared rice
grapes (optional)

Preheat oven to 425 degrees. Wrap rabbit tenderloins (or boned rabbits) with bacon strips and secure with toothpicks. Season with salt, pepper, paprika and thyme. Roll in flour and shake off excess. Put oil in hot oven-proof skillet and sear rabbits on all sides. Place in oven with apple slices on top for 10 minutes or until fully cooked. Arrange rabbit on platter with rice. Top with sauce (recipe below) and garnish with baked apple slices and grapes. Serves 6 to 8.

Sauce:

1 stick butter
2 onions, chopped
¾ pound mushrooms
3 tablespoons parsley
1 tablespoon garlic,
   chopped
⅛ teaspoon thyme
⅛ teaspoon rosemary
1 bay leaf

6 juniper berries
1 cup ginger-flavored
   currant wine
2 teaspoons salt
1 teaspoon white pepper
½ cup sour cream
½ cup half and half
2 tablespoons flour

In skillet, melt butter and sauté onions. Add mushrooms, parsley, garlic, thyme, rosemary, bay leaf and juniper berries and cook for 1 minute. Add wine, salt and pepper; bring to boil. Reduce and simmer for 5 minutes. Meanwhile, combine sour cream, half and half and flour. Whisk until smooth. Stir into sauce and simmer for 5 minutes. Serve with rabbit. Also good with chicken and veal. Serves 8.

MICHIE TAVERN
Charlottesville

MICHIE TAVERN   **H**istoric Michie Tavern was among America's first Southern taverns to feature a drive-in bar. Back in 1746, "Scotch" John Michie, exiled from Scotland for his religious beliefs, purchased more than 1,000 acres from Major John Henry, the famous orator's father. Michie developed this site, and in the late 1770s, his son William opened the Michie home as an "ordinary" where thirsty "gentleman" travelers could partake of spirits produced by E. C. Booze (hence the origin of liquor's slang term) inside the tavern's Tap Room. However, their stagecoach drivers could only be served from the outside bar on the front porch.

The outside bar is still there, and the tavern still dispenses hospitality much as it did to our early ancestors, except apple cider instead of "booze" is served in pewterlike cups.

Guests are greeted by costumed hostesses and then proceed through the log- and clay-plastered dining room to a buffet arrangement. There your plate may be filled with as much as you please of Fried Chicken, Potato Salad, Green Beans, Black-Eyed Peas, Corn Bread, Biscuits, Fruit Cobbler and the best Stewed Tomatoes in Virginia.

All the recipes are faithfully reproduced from colonial days, even the Stewed Tomatoes, which were called the "devil's apple" back then. This "apple" was thought to induce passion and was therefore forbidden, so try this recipe at your own discretion.

Either before or after dining, you may visit the historic tavern museum. It offers an authentic taste of how our ancestors prepared meals, entertained and slept at an ordinary. A copy of their rules stipulated: "Only five to a bed; no boots worn in bed; no tinkers or razor grinders allowed." I certainly concur with the "no boots" rule.

The Meadow Run Grist Mill is also included in your tour. You may browse through the old milling operation, which was moved from its original site in Laurel Hill, Virginia, and painstakingly reconstructed on its current mountaintop site. A General Store is housed at the mill, and the Virginia Wine Museum is free and is located on the second floor. The location is perfect, as it commands a breathtaking view of Charlottesville.

Michie Tavern is located on Route 53 near Monticello. Lunch is served daily from 11:15 a.m. until 3:30 p.m. in the summer and from 11:30 a.m. until 3:00 p.m. other seasons. The Spring House is open for light meals from 9:00 a.m. until 4:30 p.m. in June, July and August. Reservations are required for parties of 15 or more. The phone number is (804) 977-1234.

MICHIE TAVERN'S STEWED TOMATOES

4 cups whole tomatoes,
  peeled and quartered
½ cup sugar
¼ stick butter, melted

½ teaspoon salt
6 baked Biscuits,
  (recipe below)

In a saucepan, combine tomatoes, sugar, butter and salt. Crumble biscuits over the mixture. Cover and cook over a medium heat for 15 minutes. Serves 6.

MICHIE TAVERN'S BISCUITS

2 cups all-purpose flour
2 teaspoons baking powder
¼ teaspoon salt

3 tablespoons shortening
⅔ cup milk

Sift together flour, baking powder and salt. Add shortening and stir in milk quickly with fork, making dough light and fluffy but not sticky. Take dough and knead by hand until it is smooth, approximately 20 times. Roll out dough on lightly floured board to ½-inch thickness. Cut into biscuits. Bake on greased cookie sheet at 450 degrees for 12 to 16 minutes. Yields 14 to 16 biscuits.

MICHIE TAVERN'S COLONIAL FRIED CHICKEN

¾ cup all-purpose flour
1½ tablespoons oregano
½ teaspoon paprika
1 teaspoon garlic salt

¼ teaspoon pepper
1 2- to 3-pound fryer, cut up
3 cups shortening

Combine flour with oregano, paprika, garlic salt and pepper. Roll the chicken, piece by piece, in the mixture until well-coated. Melt shortening in heavy, cast-iron skillet or Dutch oven to 350 degrees. Fry chicken for 12 to 15 minutes on each side, or until tender. Serves 4 to 6.

MICHIE TAVERN'S APPLE COBBLER

¾ cup sugar
2 tablespoons flour, if fruit
  is juicy
⅛ teaspoon salt
½ teaspoon grated lemon
  peel
1½ teaspoons lemon juice

1 teaspoon nutmeg
½ teaspoon cinnamon
6 to 7 cooking apples,
  peeled, cored and thinly
  sliced
Pie Crust (see Index)
1 tablespoon butter

In a mixing bowl combine all ingredients except apples, pie crust and butter. Prepare pie crust and line either large oven-proof square or rectangular dish; add half of apples and sprinkle with half of sugar mixture. Top with remaining apples and remaining sugar mixture. Dot with butter. Add top crust, rolled to desired thickness. Make slits for steam to escape, and dot with more butter. Place pie in a 450-degree, preheated oven and bake for 40 to 50 minutes. Serves 15.

MILLER'S
Charlottesville

MILLER'S

As a child I could hold on to money only until I got to the store—the drugstore, that is. There, my nickel was traded for a Cherry Coke mixed to order at the soda fountain.

The day I walked into Miller's, a drugstore from 1880 until 1975, those memories came flooding back. The high, sculptured-tin ceiling, old mosaic tile floors and walls lined with rich cherry and mahogany shelves were part of my past. The soda fountain, now a bar, still retains the handsome old mirror installed by the original owner, Dr. G.T. Miller.

The current owner showed me one of Dr. Miller's own patent medicines that had made the doctor well known in Charlottesville. The medication was called "Egyptian Herb Tonic for Women." The label read, "This prescription is the favorite prescription of a Practicing Physician and is especially useful in those disorders of the system peculiar to women."

I don't wonder—the tonic contained twelve percent alcohol! The label's explanation went on: "Remember its field of usefulness begins with early adolescence and continues clear through life and old age." Does that mean old age is a stage after life? I wonder, but apparently it didn't confuse Dr. Miller's patients, or after drinking several bottles they ceased to care.

I do know that I was happy to have found this old drugstore, even if I couldn't get a Cherry Coke. Instead, I had an Italian pastry called Calzone. Naturally, I wanted the recipe for this hearty meal. It didn't remind me of Italian cooking, but it was very good, nonetheless.

I went on to sample their delicious Jambalaya, reminiscent of New Orleans, served with hot, freshly baked muffins. I finished with a serving of their heavenly Chocolate Mousse.

My meal was accompanied by music that sounded as if it came from an old player piano, but I'm told that dinner guests are treated to live jazz and blues nightly. Guests also have the option of outside dining, where alcoholic beverages can be served only during evening hours. The Mesquite Grill Dining Room is a new attraction at Miller's.

The dinner menu becomes more sophisticated, offering such dishes as Beef Bourguignon and Broiled Fish.

For those who want something different from the usual fare, nostalgic Miller's is your kind of place.

Miller's is located at 109 West Main Street in Charlottesville. Lunch is served from 11:30 a.m. until 2:00 p.m., Monday through Friday; dinner is from 5:00 p.m. until 9:30 p.m., Monday through Thursday, and from 5:00 p.m. until 10:00 p.m., Friday and Saturday. For reservations (recommended) call (804) 971-8511.

MILLER'S JAMBALAYA

2 tablespoons butter
4 slices bacon, chopped
1 large onion, chopped
1 bay leaf
½ teaspoon thyme
2 16-ounce cans peeled
tomatoes
3 cloves garlic, chopped
¼ green bell pepper,
chopped

1 tablespoon Worcestershire
sauce
dash of Tabasco sauce
¼ teaspoon cayenne
salt and pepper to taste
3 cups rice (follow package
directions)
2 cups chicken, cooked
1 pound medium shrimp,
cleaned

Melt butter in large Dutch oven and sauté bacon, onions, bay leaf and thyme. Lower heat and add tomatoes and cook 5 minutes. Add garlic, green pepper, Worcestershire sauce, Tabasco sauce, cayenne, salt and pepper. Cook for 30 minutes, stirring frequently. Meanwhile, prepare rice in separate saucepan. Stir in chicken and cook for 5 minutes. About 7 minutes before serving, stir in rice and shrimp. Serves 8.

MILLER'S CHOCOLATE MOUSSE

3 eggs, separated
4½ ounces chocolate chips

1¼ cups whipped cream
1 tablespoon creme de cacao

Separate yolks from whites of eggs (reserving whites) and set aside. Melt chocolate in saucepan over low heat, add yolks. Stir until well blended; cool. Whip cream and fold in cooled chocolate/egg mixture with creme de cacao. In separate bowl, beat egg whites until stiff and gently fold into chocolate cream mixture. Pour into 8 individual molds or one 2½-quart mold. Chill until set. May garnish with additional whipped cream if desired. Serves 8.

MILLER'S CALZONE

Pastry:

3 cups all-purpose flour	⅓ cup margarine
1 cup whole wheat flour	⅓ cup shortening
1¼ tablespoons salt	buttermilk as needed

In mixing bowl, measure flour and salt together. Quarter margarine and shortening into cubes and add to bowl. Work the dough by hand, adding buttermilk a tablespoon at a time until kneaded to a pliable dough consistency. Cover and refrigerate.

Filling:

1½ cups Ricotta cheese	¼ teaspoon thyme
¼ cup Parmesan cheese	1 egg, beaten
salt and pepper to taste	1 cup ham, diced

In mixing bowl, combine all ingredients. Take dough and divide it into 6 equal balls. On floured surface, roll out dough to ¼-inch thickness. Place ⅙ of filling mixture on dough and fold dough in half, forming a half-moon shape. Pinch edges together and prick dough with a fork. Repeat until all are filled. Place on greased baking sheet and bake in a 350-degree oven approximately 20 minutes. Serves 6.

SILVER THATCH INN
Charlottesville

SILVER THATCH INN

If, after dining, you spend the night in the upstairs front bedroom, there's a chance that the ghost of a Hessian soldier will playfully snatch the pillow from beneath your sleeping head and toss it across the room. At least this was true before the new owners of the Silver Thatch Inn remodeled the rooms into comfortable, antique-filled remembrances of another time.

Yes, in addition to haute cuisine, the Silver Thatch has its ghost. This spirit reportedly was a German soldier, one of many captured by General Horatio Gage in the 1777 Battle of Saratoga. The Hessians were marched to Virginia, where they were forced to build a penal facility to house themselves. That facility is now a part of the present structure of the Silver Thatch Inn. During the Hessians' imprisonment, one of the soldiers died, and his spirit seems to delight in playing pranks on the inn's caretakers.

I tried to talk my daughter Daintry into sleeping in the front upstairs bedroom on the premise that spirits won't appear to me because they know I'll write about them. Her reply was a terse, "Bag it!" However, the next morning she did try to open a tiny closet in that room. The previous owners had told me that the closet's door will open and close at will when the ghost is active, but can't be opened otherwise. Daintry couldn't open the door but reported feeling a strange coldness surrounding the closet.

Daintry later told me she had considered snatching my pillow in the night, but decided against the prank, figuring I'd "freak out." Nor did she want to ruin our pleasant memories of the excellent time and meal we enjoyed at the inn.

For dinner, I had the wonderful Lamb with Mint Sauce. Daintry was particularly delighted by a couple of the vegetable dishes, Spaghetti Squash and Mushrooms Albemarle, a spicy concoction with pork sausage, red pepper, onion and garlic. Our meals were not exactly low-calorie ones, but if that had been our intent we could have dined on any number of broiled fish dishes, including their Blackened Redfish, and substituted the romantic atmosphere of this beautiful restaurant for dessert.

The Silver Thatch Inn is located at 3001 Hollymead Drive in Charlottesville. Dinner is served to the public Tuesday through Saturday from 5:30 p.m. until 9:00 p.m. Breakfast is served to lodging guests daily. For reservations (recommended) call (804) 978-4686.

SILVER THATCH INN'S SPAGHETTI SQUASH

1 large spaghetti squash
3 to 4 tablespoons butter
12 fresh mushrooms, sliced thin
2 medium zucchini, sliced thin
2 medium tomatoes, seeded and diced
salt and pepper to taste
1 cup parmesan, fontina or mild cheese, shredded
dollop or more sweet butter

Cook spaghetti squash in a 5-quart Dutch oven or large pot for 1½ hours on a medium to slow boil, adding water as needed. In a sauté skillet, melt the butter and stir in mushrooms, zucchini and tomatoes. Stir continuously until vegetables are tender. Slice spaghetti squash in half and remove seeds. Scoop out spaghetti and place in a lightly greased 2-quart casserole. Add vegetables, salt, pepper and cheese and mix until combined. Heat in a warm oven and serve with a dollop of butter if desired. Serves 4 to 6.

SILVER THATCH INN'S MUSHROOMS ALBEMARLE

12 very large mushroom
  caps
1 tablespoon olive oil
1 pound pork sausage
1 green pepper, diced
1/2 red pepper, diced
1/2 medium red onion, diced

1 1/2 teaspoons fresh garlic,
  minced
1/4 cup parmesan cheese,
  grated
1/2 cup fontina cheese,
  grated

Preheat oven to 400 degrees. Cook mushrooms in a large skillet until barely tender. In a large sauté pan, heat olive oil on high and crumble sausage into pan a little at a time. Stir until sausage loses pink color. Add vegetables and garlic and sauté until barely tender. Place mushroom caps in a lightly greased 8- to 10-inch shallow casserole. Add sausage and vegetable mixture and top with cheeses. Bake for 15 minutes. Serves 6 to 8.

SILVER THATCH INN'S MINT SAUCE

1/2 cup sugar
1/4 cup white wine vinegar
1/4 cup water

1 10-ounce jar mint jelly
1 cup fresh mint leaves,
  chopped

In a small saucepan, mix sugar, vinegar and water over medium heat. Add mint jelly and stir to incorporate. When jelly dissolves, add mint leaves. Serve over lamb loin or lamb chops. Do not let sauce cool, as it will harden. Serves 4 or more.

THE BOAR'S HEAD INN
Charlottesville

THE BOAR'S HEAD INN

Eating dinner without a fork? Impossible, you say. It's possible and it happens each year at the Festival Before Forks, a sixteenth-century English banquet celebrated during Christmastime at the Boar's Head Inn. I'm told that some guests try to sneak in forks, but the strict rules require a humorous confiscation of the utensils.

Merrymaking abounds here under the "Lord of Misrule," where festivities include mumming (a Medieval word for dancing), wassailing, caroling and the performing of plays and music. This is definitely the place to enjoy Christmas if you're into fun and frolic, but there's something going on at this reconstructed 1834 gristmill any time of the year.

Their most famous dining room is the Old Mill Room, crowned with the original fourteen-inch thick, heart pine rough-hewn beams. This rustic room is softened with cornflower blue linen cloths and white carnations at each table. Beyond this dining area is a light and airy garden room overlooking a pond of mallards and visiting geese. My choice of dining, however, is outside beneath a gigantic sycamore, which is romantically lighted for evening diners.

Downstairs in the dining room, a band plays everything from old swing tunes to popular classics.

I sampled most of their entrées. Their preparation of Virginia Ham is superb. The usual salty taste is ameliorated by the Raisin Sauce. The best Caesar Salad I've ever tasted is prepared tableside. Their research indicates that this unique salad is Mexican in origin. Diners will also enjoy a variety of fresh desserts prepared daily in their own bakery.

The Boar's Head is particularly proud of their strong wine list, which offers a full variety of Virginia, California and imported selections.

If you visit in the warmer seasons you can go ballooning on one of their champagne balloon flights. Sounds a bit heady for me; I'm much more inclined toward their hedonistic romp at Christmas.

The Boar's Head Inn is located three miles from Charlottesville on Highway 250 West. Breakfast is served Monday through Friday from 7:00 a.m. until 10:30 a.m., and on Saturday and Sunday from 7:30 p.m. until 10:30 a.m. Lunch is served daily from noon until 2:00 p.m. and dinner from 6:00 p.m. until 9:30 p.m. except on Sunday, when the inn closes at 8:30 p.m. Sunday brunch is served from 10:00 a.m. until 2:30 p.m. Jackets are required for gentlemen dining in the Old Mill Room. For reservations (required for dinner) call (804) 296-2181.

BOAR'S HEAD INN'S VIRGINIA HAM WITH RAISIN SAUCE

1 16- to 18-pound ham   **1 16-ounce can of peach halves**

Cover ham with water and soak overnight. Drain water and place ham in a large pot and cover with cold water. Bring to a simmer and cook for 2 to 3 hours, or until bone removes easily. Drain water and remove fat rind. Bake at 375 degrees for 45 minutes, glazing with juice from peaches. Garnish with peach halves and serve with Raisin Sauce (recipe below). Serves 12.

Raisin Sauce:
1 quart water	**1 cup cold water**
½ cup seedless raisins	**1 teaspoon salt**
2 oranges, juice only	**1 cup brown sugar**
1 lemon, juice only	**2 tablespoons cider vinegar**
4 tablespoons cornstarch	

Fill a saucepan with 1 quart of water and add raisins. Simmer slowly until raisins are soft. Set aside. Combine orange and lemon juices and dissolve the cornstarch in this mixture with 1 cup of water. Add the cornstarch mixture to raisin mixture; cook, stirring with a wooden spoon, until thickened and glossy. Add salt, brown sugar and vinegar. Bring to a boil, remove from heat and serve with ham.

BOAR'S HEAD INN'S
BREAST OF CHICKEN EDNAM

4 8-ounce boneless chicken
  breasts
½ cup butter or margarine
8 ounces fresh watercress
4 ounces Boursin cheese

½ pint heavy whipping
  cream
6 ounces baby shrimp or 4
jumbo shrimp, cooked

Place chicken breasts in a medium-hot skillet with melted butter or margarine. Sauté chicken on both sides, lower heat and cook until slightly brown. In a small saucepan, blanch the watercress and remove. Melt cheese in the top of a double boiler with the whipping cream, stirring all the while. Reduce heat to simmer and stir until well-blended and hot. Place chicken on a warm plate and top each breast generously with sauce. Garnish with watercress, top with shrimp and serve. Serves 4.

THE IVY INN
Charlottesville

THE IVY INN

Uncle Sam is the real benefactor of higher prices. This is why The Ivy Inn's former owner, Jean Abbott, preferred to pass the price savings on to her customers whenever possible. "After all," stated Abbot, "I don't even know Uncle Sam!" That is why I found my special champagne to be priced a good five dollars less at this beguiling restaurant than I could find it elsewhere.

Built as a farmhouse in 1863, this appealing, red brick structure sits in front of the original five-cent toll turnpike. The house is surrounded with brightly colored flowers and looks as if it were someone's home. Once inside and in the care of current owners Barbara Shifflett and David Elkins, you are treated as if you'd just dropped in for a meal at a friend's house.

Sitting in one of the downstairs dining rooms amidst a warm colonial décor, my daughter and I ordered their Champagne Melon Soup. What an appetizing way to begin a meal! Actually, the taste reminded me of a fancy champagne cocktail, with a somewhat stronger emphasis on fruit than wine.

Our appetizer was followed by a Spinach Salad with a most unusual warm and delicate dressing. Daintry tried the Chicken Pecan Waffle. This is a unique concoction of creamed chicken served over waffles and pecans, then garnished with spiced peaches and watermelon. I had to sample more than one bite of this scrumptious dish because one taste begged another.

We switched plates so Daintry could test my Scallop and Shrimp Casserole. We agree that this is a dish to please the taste buds of gourmet seafood lovers. Accompanying our lunch was a small loaf of freshly baked Sally Lunn Bread.

If trying to flatter your weight scale, you could enjoy either the Veal Supreme or their Steamed Lobster, Clams, Crab Legs and Shrimp served on a bed of greens.

Aside from its delicious cuisine, The Ivy Inn is also noted for its relaxing atmosphere. In fact, the atmosphere is so relaxing that an elderly couple have been known to take naps between courses during their weekly dinner of salad, half an entree each, half a carafe of wine and dessert.

Our dining experience was pleasantly concluded with hot Pecan Pie topped with whipped cream. The pie became a must for the recipe section. And on reflection, dining at The Ivy Inn is a must for anyone who appreciates good food in a congenial and unhurried atmosphere.

The Ivy Inn is located at 2244 Old Ivy Road in Charlottesville. Lunch is served from 11:30 a.m. until 2:00 p.m. Monday through Friday, and dinner is served from 5:00 p.m. until 9:30 p.m. Monday through Saturday. Sunday brunch is served from 11:30 a.m. until 2:00 p.m. For reservations (recommended), call (804) 977-1222.

THE IVY INN'S PECAN PIE

3 eggs, beaten
1 cup dark corn syrup
½ cup sugar
½ teaspoon salt

1 teaspoon vanilla
1 cup pecan pieces or halves
1 8-inch unbaked pie shell

In bowl, combine all ingredients, except pecans, and beat well by hand until thoroughly combined. Place pecans in unbaked pie shell and pour liquid ingredients over top. Bake at 375 degrees for 45 minutes or until set. May serve with vanilla ice cream or whipped cream, if desired. Yields 1 pie.

THE IVY INN'S SCALLOP AND
SHRIMP CASSEROLE

2 tablespoons butter
1 pound medium shrimp, cleaned
1 pound scallops
½ cup white wine
½ pound fresh mushrooms, sliced (or 1 small can of mushrooms)
1 10¾-ounce can cream of celery soup

1 cup sour cream
8 ounces sharp Cheddar cheese, grated
salt and pepper to taste
1 tablespoon Old Bay Seasoning
wild rice (follow package directions)

In skillet place butter and sauté shrimp and scallops until shrimp begin to turn pink and curl. Add wine, reduce heat to medium and cook for 2 minutes. Remove shrimp and scallops and set aside. Reduce heat to low; combine remaining ingredients, except rice, and add to skillet. Stir until well blended. Add shrimp and scallops and heat through. Serve over prepared wild rice. Serves 8 to 10.

THE IVY INN'S CHAMPAGNE MELON SOUP

⅛ of large watermelon, chopped
1 cantaloupe, chopped
juice of ½ lime
juice of ½ lemon
1 cup orange juice
1½ tablespoons honey
2 cups champagne

Chill bowls several hours before serving. Reserve a cup of watermelon and a cup of cantaloupe for garnish. Combine all ingredients, except champagne, and place in blender. Blend until puréed. Pour ¼ cup of champagne in each chilled bowl; add puréed mixture and top with watermelon and cantaloupe. Garnish with mint leaves or whipped cream, if desired. Serves 8.

THE VIRGINIAN
Charlottesville

THE VIRGINIAN During the depression, people found that it was important to indulge the human spirit in small but special ways. One very nourishing way, for both soul and body, was an occasional visit to Charlottesville's oldest downtown restaurant, The Virginian.

Established in 1921 across from the University of Virginia, this quaint college hangout of yesteryear was often mentioned on the popular TV program, *The Waltons*. How often John Boy actually visited the restaurant is unknown, but the fact that it was a popular retreat, even in depression years, attests to its fine food and casual atmosphere.

Today, old-fashioned fans hang from a white-latticed ceiling that sets off the dark wood halls and private booths.

I was quite surprised to discover that the menu did not reflect what I would have expected to be typical fare for college students, but then I also learned that while the restaurant is frequented by a youngish clientele, only about a third of them are students.

A spicy yet hearty bean soup called Caldo Gallego was a marvelous way to tease my taste buds, along with a wonderful light luncheon entrée (or appetizer) made with shrimp, tomatoes, Feta cheese and fresh basil. I washed it all down with a red Bordeaux wine.

If you are in the mood for something lighter than their luncheon burgers and Mexican dishes, you could have a special vegetarian dish for either lunch or dinner.

The dessert that seemed just the right accompaniment for my spicy meal was their Almond Custard, but don't think I didn't have a go at their Chocolate Pecan Pie. It's a fat day indeed when I pass up chocolate.

When visiting for an evening meal you might want to try one of their special fish or chicken dinners, along with an inventive cocktail dreamed up at the bar.

On a lazy weekend, think of stopping by for brunch and investigate their Eggs Chesapeake. This dish is sautéed crabmeat and tomatoes served on an English muffin and topped with a poached egg and Hollandaise sauce.

The Virginian is a restaurant that doesn't rely on old stand-bys, but prefers to create and experiment with new dishes on a daily basis. And that plays a big part in the fun of going there.

The Virginian is located at 1521 West Main Street in Charlottesville. Meals are served from 9:00 a.m. until 11:00 p.m. daily, with a late-night menu from 11:00 p.m. until 2:00 a.m., when the restaurant closes. Brunch is served from 10:00 a.m. until 3:00 p.m. on Saturday and Sunday. Reservations are not accepted, but the phone number is (804) 293-2606.

THE VIRGINIAN'S CHOCOLATE PECAN PIE

¼ pound or 1 stick melted
  butter
1¼ cups brown sugar
1¼ cups light corn syrup
5 eggs

1½ teaspoons vanilla
1 tablespoon rum
1 9-inch pie shell
¾ cup chocolate chips
1 cup pecan halves

Cream butter and brown sugar thoroughly with electric mixer; gradually add corn syrup. Beat in eggs, one at a time. Add vanilla and rum. Sprinkle pie shell with chocolate chips and pecans. Pour in filling. Bake at 350 degrees until set, about 40 to 50 minutes. Yields 1 pie.

THE VIRGINIAN'S FETA, BASIL, SHRIMP & TOMATO PASTA SAUCE

1 pound tiny shrimp,
  cleaned
juice of ½ a lemon
water to cover shrimp
4 tomatoes, peeled, cored
  and chopped
10 fresh basil leaves,
  chopped

½ medium onion, chopped
¾ cup olive oil
5 ounces Feta cheese
linguine or fettucine
  noodles (follow package
  directions)

Poach shrimp in saucepan with lemon and water about 1 to 2 minutes. Remove, drain and cool. In separate container, combine tomatoes, basil leaves, onion and olive oil and stir thoroughly. Add cooled shrimp and Feta cheese. Serve over linguine or fettucine noodles. Serves 6 to 8.

THE VIRGINIAN'S CALDO GALLEGO
(BEAN SOUP)

1 pound pinto beans
2 quarts water
8 strips bacon
1 pound bulk sausage
1½ medium onions, thinly sliced
5 garlic cloves, chopped
1 16-ounce can whole peeled tomatoes
1 can chicken broth or stock

3 carrots, thinly sliced
3 potatoes, peeled and thinly sliced
1 teaspoon pepper
1 teaspoon salt or to taste
2 bay leaves
1 10-ounce package frozen spinach
¼ cup white wine

Soak beans overnight in water in large soup kettle. The next day bring water to boil and reduce heat to simmer. Cook until beans are tender, about 6 to 8 hours. Meanwhile, cook bacon; set aside and reserve bacon drippings. In separate pan, sauté sausage by crumbling as it is added to pan and turning until done but not browned. Drain sausage. Sauté onions and garlic in bacon drippings. Drain. When beans are tender, add all other ingredients except spinach and wine. Simmer until potatoes and carrots are tender, about an hour. During the last 15 minutes, add spinach and wine. More chicken broth may be added for a thinner soup. Serves 12 generously.

PROSPECT HILL
Trevilians

PROSPECT HILL

Author Margaret Mitchell could have been writing about Prospect Hill in *Gone With The Wind*. The spring morning that I drove past the boxwood hedge I glimpsed the Manor House through the English tree garden, wreathed in a pastel coiffure of blossoming dogwoods. The 1732 house, now surrounded by renovated slave quarters, was originally converted from a barn when the Roger Thompson family's log cabin burned. The following year, Richmond Terrill took over the property and began shaping it into a plantation. When William Overton purchased it in 1840, two additional wings and a spiral staircase were added to the frame home.

After the Civil War, Prospect Hill faced a dilemma that was common among plantations. Fortunately, the house was not burned, but the plantation had to function without labor or capital. For sixteen years the Overtons eked out a subsistance, then finally, taking the cue from other plantations, opened their home to guests. Thus, for over one hundred years this home has maintained the integrity of genteel hospitality that the South seems to have patented. True Southern hospitality is endangered these days and too often supplanted with phony substitutions.

"Prospect Hill is small," explains owner, Bill Sheehan, and its very smallness helps him, his wife, Mireille, and their son, Michael, combat the mediocrity they have experienced in too many other so-called "Southern" settings.

It is Mireille's French heritage that is aromatically detected from the kitchen, where the primary focus is on preparing fresh food naturally.

Overnight guests can either have breakfast in bed or dine in the blue and white colonial breakfast room, after Bill clangs the bell. The meal is always a surprise. That morning freshly squeezed orange juice arrived in a wine glass, followed by fried Apple Fritter Pancakes and coffee. Guests from distant states joined me in appreciation of this perfectly executed meal. They also offered satisfied remarks about their previous night's dinner of Onion Soup, Salad Vinaigrette and continental-style Roast Beef served with Red Potatoes and Asparagus, ending with a Strawberry Cream Torte.

Each evening at the set-priced meal, guests may purchase either a Virginia or French wine to enhance the meal.

The restaurant operates in a mode similar to that of a family. Meals are designed by the family head and substitutions (say, for dieters) are accommodated. They won't force you to eat something you hate, as your mother did, but choices are limited. This has never been a deterrent, as guests enjoy the element of surprise.

Chefs in the region told me that they chose to dine at Prospect Hill on their nights off. What better compliment can be paid?

Prospect Hill is located near Zion Crossroads on Route 613 in Trevilians. Dinner is served at 7:00 p.m. Monday through Thursday, at 8:00 p.m. on Friday and Saturday and at 6:00 p.m. on Sunday. Breakfast is served to lodging guests only. For reservations (required) call (703) 967-0844.

PROSPECT HILL'S FRITTATA ZUCCHINI

1 pound zucchini or yellow squash	6 eggs
	½ cup Mozzarella cheese

Peel zucchini and shred, using largest hole in grater or food processor. Grease a 12-inch by 16-inch oven-proof dish or casserole and place shredded zucchini on bottom. Beat eggs and pour over zucchini. Sprinkle shredded cheese over top and bake in top third of 350-degree oven until lightly browned, about 30 to 40 minutes. Serves 4 to 6.

PROSPECT HILL'S APPLE FRITTER PANCAKES

Pancake Batter:

3 eggs

⅔ cup all-purpose flour

1 cup milk

1 tablespoon sugar

1 teaspoon baking soda

1 teaspoon baking powder

2 tablespoons vegetable oil

In blender or with electric beater, combine all ingredients except oil and blend until smooth. (Let set 10 to 15 minutes for a thin batter.)

Add oil to skillet and swirl to coat bottom over medium-high heat. Pour or ladle batter into desired size of pancake (1½ to 3 tablespoons) and cook until edges are lightly browned. Turn pancake to cook other side. Repeat until all batter is used, stacking pancakes on a dish. Keep warm in 150-degree oven.

12 slices bacon

2 to 3 medium-sized apples

2 tablespoons butter

1 teaspoon lemon juice or vinegar

Fry bacon in large cast-iron skillet and set bacon aside. Drain skillet and reserve drippings. Peel and slice apples ¼-inch thick and chop coarsely. Place in bowl of cold water with lemon juice or vinegar and set aside for 5 to 10 minutes. Drain apples, drying them with a paper towel. Add about 2 tablespoons of the bacon drippings and the butter to a clean skillet and heat over medium-high heat, swirling drippings and butter until well combined. Sauté apples for 2 to 3 minutes until lightly browned, being careful not to overcook. Remove from pan. Place 2 or more tablespoons of cooked apples on each pancake and roll up and keep warm in oven until ready to serve. Serve with bacon. Yields 12 to 16 pancakes, depending on size.

BAVARIAN CHEF
Madison

BAVARIAN CHEF

A soup to cure sinus? You've got to be kidding. But a sampling of Hungarian Goulash Soup created by Chef Jerome Thalwitz made a believer out of me.

I stumbled upon this medical discovery quite by accident. My Virginia friends had told me about this restaurant, described by *The New York Times* as offering "one of the best German meals available anywhere." Therefore, on my last trip to Virginia, I scheduled a detour.

Upon arrival, my daughter Daintry was suffering with sinus problems. When Thalwitz realized her discomfort, a special soup was suggested to alleviate her condition. When the steaming bowl arrived, Daintry's wan smile wore an edge of uncertainty, but politely, she began to sample. After a couple of spoonfuls, she interrupted my conversation with Thalwitz demanding, "Mother, get this recipe!" She was so insistent that another bowl of their delicious, magical potion was brought for me.

My friends did not know about this soup when they recommended the restaurant. They had raved about the Mandelschnitzel, which I discovered is pork baked in a wonderful strawberry and gin sauce. The unusual combination makes the dish superb.

If doing a calorie cheat, try their Filet Mignon or Zwiebelbraten, a roast beef cooked in beer and onions.

They offer a wine list that is neither extravagant nor pretentious, but skillfully designed to complement the food. Actually, there is not an ounce of pretense in this Bavarian-American restaurant.

The upstairs has the appearance of an old Bavarian inn, with its wood beams and German décor, while the downstairs features a large mural of Southern Bavaria. It was while sitting opposite this rendering of a famous Bavarian castle that we concluded our meal with a Grand Marnier Creme Torte that could provoke hazardous driving. For authentic Bavarian food with a creative touch, try this old converted truck stop. Some truck stop!

The Bavarian Chef is located on Highway 29, about 5 miles south of Madison. Dinner is served Monday through Saturday from 4:30 p.m. until 10:00 p.m. Meals are served from 11:30 a.m. until 10:00 p.m. on Sunday. For reservations (required) call (703) 948-6505.

BAVARIAN CHEF'S GRAND MARNIER CREME TORTE

12 ounces sweet chocolate
2 sticks margarine
½ cup cocoa
½ cup sugar

1 ounce brandy
1 ounce light rum
graham cracker crust in
   9-inch pan, baked

In a saucepan over medium heat, melt chocolate and margarine. Stir in cocoa and sugar. When combined, add brandy and rum and mix thoroughly. Pour mixture into graham cracker crust and freeze.

Cream Filling:
6 egg yolks
⅓ cup sugar
1 cup whipping cream

½ cup Grand Marnier (or to
   taste)

With electric mixer, combine egg yolks and sugar and beat until mixture doubles. Put in refrigerator until chilled. Whip cream and slowly fold cream into sugar mixture. Slowly add Grand Marnier. Pour on top of first layer and freeze. Cover with plastic wrap. Yields one torte.

BAVARIAN CHEF'S MANDELSCHNITZEL

2 eggs
2 cups fine bread crumbs
2 ounces blanched almonds,
   sliced

4 6-ounce pork tenderloins
flour for dredging
3 tablespoons butter

Beat eggs. In separate bowl, combine bread crumbs and almonds. Lightly dredge pork in flour. Dip in egg batter, and roll in bread crumb mixture to cover. Melt 3 tablespoons butter in large skillet and sauté pork until golden brown on both sides. Remove from pan, place on platter and keep warm. Serves 4.

Sauce:

2 tablespoons butter
1 small onion, chopped
1 cup chicken stock or broth
5 ounces strawberry
 preserves
2 tablespoons sugar
1 ounce gin

1 ounce kirschwasser (or
 kirsch)
¼ cup cornstarch
¾ cup water
cayenne to taste
1 lemon, sliced

Melt 2 tablespoons butter in skillet and sauté onions until soft. Add chicken stock, strawberry preserves, sugar, gin and kirschwasser. Mix cornstarch and ¾ cup water in cup and stir until cornstarch is dissolved. Add to sauce and stir thickened. Sprinkle with cayenne to taste. Place sauce on warmed plates and lay pork on top. Garnish with lemon slices. Serves 4.

BAVARIAN CHEF'S HUNGARIAN GOULASH SOUP

4 sticks margarine
1 pound top round steak,
 cut into bite-size pieces
2 large onions, chopped
¼ cup ground beef
2 lemon peels, finely grated
2 tablespoons caraway seeds
1 tablespoon garlic salt

3 tablespoons Hungarian
 paprika (no substitutes)
2 bay leaves
2 cups beef stock
white pepper and salt to
 taste
cayenne to taste
2 tablespoons flour
½ cup water

In heavy Dutch oven, melt margarine as needed and sauté steak, onions and ground beef. Reduce heat and add lemon peels, caraway seeds, garlic salt, Hungarian paprika, bay leaves and beef stock. Simmer over medium heat for at least 1 hour. Add salt, white pepper and cayenne to taste. Mix flour in half a cup of water and add to mixture. Stir until soup thickens slightly. Serves 10 to 12.

THE CONYERS HOUSE
Sperryville

THE CONYERS HOUSE

The day we arrived at the Conyers House, the spring weather was perfect, but I had the feeling that if the weather had been poor, innkeepers Norman and Sandra Cartwright-Brown could have rectified the atmosphere. No, they do not control the weather, but they do set the tone in their restored 1770 home. Sandra, the only Rappahannock County hostess who rides the hunt, was wearing horseback-riding attire. She lit a fire in the stone fireplace in the living room, which had been part of Conyers General Store in the late 1800s. A grand piano, bedecked with family photographs and a huge bouquet of fragrant lilacs, stood at one end of the room. With its bookshelves and its view of the beautiful, rolling hillside, it had the country, rustic look of *House Beautiful*.

Once I was comfortable in an antique rocker, sherry, cheeses, caviar and a plate of Ham Swirls were set upon a nearby coffee table. After I'd tasted one of the delicious Ham Swirls, I asked for the recipe. Sandra laughed and said, "You don't want that—it's too simple." But I convinced her that anything so tasty and so simple is worthy of any cook's repertoire.

A tour before dinner included a stop in the cellar room that had been converted from the home's original kitchen to a cozy guest bedroom complete with antiques, a fireplace, eighteen-inch-thick stone walls and a lovely view. On our tour, Sandra also told me that the General Store had once been owned by Pascal Manafe Finks, who engaged in moneylending. The story goes that Finks insisted that borrowers put up their land as collateral for loans. When one borrower repaid his debt too promptly, Finks remarked, "If I'd knowed you was gonna pay me back, I never would have lent it to you in the first place!"

Our candlelight dinner was served in the pale green dining room, which features antique china, silver and crystal. Dinner began with a soup seasoned with locally picked morels that bestowed a woodsy taste and aroma. To announce the end of a course, guests ring a little crystal dinner bell that delighted my companion, Judy Plough. A light, crisp Radicchio Salad followed. Then came our delicious, fresh Mountain Trout enhanced with Conyers's own corn bread and broccoli. This corn bread with whole corn kernels rings its own bell. Dessert came in two stages. At our table, we were served a very light Lemon Mousse. Half an hour later in the kitchen, while polishing a pair of borrowed riding boots for my morning trail ride, I was given a taste of their wonderful Parsnip Cake—a fitting finale to a casual yet elegant evening.

The Conyers House is located outside Sperryville on Slate Mill Road (Route 707). Depending upon the season, breakfast is served either at a single 9:00 a.m. seating or at both 8:30 a.m. and 10:00 a.m. Dinner is served at 8:00 p.m. daily. For reservations (required 24 to 48 hours in advance) call (703) 987-8025.

CONYERS HOUSE'S HAM SWIRLS

1 package crescent roll dough

2 or more tablespoons Dijon mustard

4 to 6 slices mozzarella cheese

4 to 6 slices ham, sliced thin

Grease a cookie sheet and place dough on sheet, pinching the corners to form a rectangle. Spread dough generously with mustard. Place cheese slices on top of mustard until dough is covered. Place ham slices on top of cheese. Roll up dough like a jelly roll. Cut roll into ¼-inch slices. Place slices on sheet and bake at 375 degrees for 20 minutes. Serves 4.

CONYERS HOUSE'S LEMON MOUSSE

1½ tablespoons unflavored
  gelatin
½ cup water
2¼ cups sugar
1 cup water

1 cup fresh lemon juice
⅔ cup heavy cream
4 egg whites
zest of 1 lemon

Place electric mixer bowl and beaters in freezer to chill. Place gelatin and ½ cup water in a second mixer bowl or a food processor bowl and let stand for 10 minutes. In a saucepan, combine 1¾ cups of the sugar with 1 cup water. Add lemon juice and bring to a boil, stirring to dissolve. Boil 1 minute. Add half of hot lemon syrup to gelatin mixture and mix until combined. Remove bowl and place in freezer until mixture cools. Place remaining hot lemon syrup in a small bowl and set in a bed of ice. Remove electric mixer bowl and beaters from freezer and whip cream until peaks form. Set aside in refrigerator. Clean beaters. In electric mixer, beat egg whites until soft peaks form. Add remaining ½ cup sugar and beat until stiff peaks form. When lemon syrup in ice bed is the consistency of heavy cream, remove second bowl from freezer and add lemon syrup and gelatin mixture. Mix in electric mixer or food processor, turning on and off rapidly until incorporated. Transfer mixture to a large bowl and gently fold in half of beaten egg whites. Fold in whipping cream and remaining half of egg whites. Refrigerate in a large covered bowl for at least 30 minutes. Garnish with zest of 1 lemon. Serves 8 to 10.

CONYERS HOUSE'S MOUNTAIN TROUT

2 fresh mountain trout
3 to 4 tablespoons butter

3 tablespoons fresh parsley
seasoned salt to taste

Clean trout, leaving head, and sauté in a skillet of melted butter. Add parsley and seasoned salt. Sauté on each side about 2 minutes. Remove from skillet and wrap in aluminum foil. Place on baking sheet and bake in a 250-degree oven for 30 minutes. Serves 2.

SIXTY-SEVEN WATERLOO
Warrenton

SIXTY-SEVEN
WATERLOO

Can you imagine spending eighty hours refinishing an 1838 spindle-style mantel? That was just one of the projects undertaken by Philip and Alison Harway when they purchased the antebellum mansion built by General Eppa Hunton at number Sixty-Seven Waterloo. Today a portrait of the general, acclaimed at Gettysburg and elected to Congress in 1873, hangs above this mantel.

In 1908, the home became the residence of artist Richard Brooke, who was appointed vice-principal of the School of Art at the Corcoran in Washington. Miraculously, the home escaped the Great Fire of 1909 that destroyed not only Brooke's studio and valuable art collection but the entire western part of Warrenton.

After many months of renovating the original wood floors and walls and tracing down the family portraits that now hang in the upstairs sitting room and stairway, the Harways opened a restaurant serving traditional French cuisine. This success led them to transform the original slave quarters at the back of the home into a rustic wood tavern, whimsically named Napoleon's.

It was one of those heaven-sent, clear spring days when I dined on their outdoor patio above Napoleon's. That meal was my special event of the day, as it is the philosophy of the Harways that eating must be more than a habit to satisfy basic needs. True exponents of culinary art were placed before me.

The spectacle began with a subtle, creamy Mousse de Foie (goose liver) and a spicy Green Peppercorn Pâté served on their homebaked Honey Whole Wheat Bread and crackers. I selected an unpretentious white chardonnay from one of their bimonthly wine tastings, which proved the right choice for my own taste-testing of their saucy Crabmeat with Hazelnuts, a homemade Pasta stuffed with herbs and cheeses and the best Asparagus on Puff Pastry that I've tasted.

Then came the dessert masterpieces. The Chocolate Amaretto Mousse fashioned into tiers of ruffled chocolate lace looked as if it should have been framed rather than devoured. This sinfully succulent creation competed with a Strawberry Charlotte that artistically tucked a mousse into its center.

This restaurant takes such pleasure in presentation that they welcome the challenge (when notified in advance) to prepare diet menus that deliver the same appeal as their more affluent dishes.

Sixty-Seven Waterloo is located in Warrenton at Sixty-seven Waterloo Street. Dinner is served from 5:30 p.m. until 10:00 p.m. Tuesday through Sunday. For reservations (recommended) call (703) 347-1200.

SIXTY-SEVEN WATERLOO'S
ACORN SQUASH BISQUE

10 medium-sized acorn
   squash
3 tablespoons butter
2 white leeks, chopped fine
2 cups chicken stock
1 quart heavy cream

salt and pepper to taste
half-and-half cream, if
   desired
parsley for garnish
1 cup Parmesan cheese
1 cup croutons

Cut tops off 6 squash and clean insides; remove flesh and reserve both flesh and shells. Remove and reserve flesh from the 4 remaining squash, discarding the shells. Melt butter in a skillet and add the leeks, cooking over medium-low heat for 3 to 4 minutes. Cut squash flesh into tiny pieces, add to leeks and stir. Add chicken stock, cream, salt and pepper. Cook over low heat until squash is tender, stirring often. If the bisque becomes too thick, thin with a little half-and-half cream. Cut bottoms from the 6 squash shells to stabilize on plates. Ladle bisque into shells and garnish with equal amounts of parsley, cheese and croutons. Serves 6.

SIXTY-SEVEN WATERLOO'S DUCK BREAST

1 duck breast
dash of salt
1 tablespoon vegetable oil
1 tablespoon butter
1 minced shallot
1/4 cup white wine
1/8 cup cognac
1 to 2 tablespoons green
  peppercorns

4 ounces veal stock (recipe
  follows)
2 ounces heavy cream
salt to taste
1 tablespoon butter, cut
  into bits
1/2 cup sliced mushrooms,
  sautéed
parsley

Skin duck and salt lightly. Place on grill and roast until medium-rare. Remove and keep warm. In a saucepan, heat oil and butter and cook shallot until light brown. Add wine and cognac and stir in peppercorns. Add veal stock and cook until sauce is reduced to half. Stir in cream and check seasoning. Salt to taste and stir in bits of butter until flavors are well-blended. Split duck and arrange on plates. Ladle sauce over top and garnish with mushrooms and parsley. Serves 2.

SIXTY-SEVEN WATERLOO'S VEAL STOCK

3 pounds veal bones
1 1/2 pounds raw veal shank
  or veal trimmings
3 carrots, sliced
2 medium onions, chopped
1 celery rib, sliced
  diagonally

1 clove garlic, chopped
2 bay leaves
6 sprigs parsley
pinch of thyme
2 teaspoons salt
1/2 teaspoon pepper

Crack bones by heating in hot oven for half an hour or longer. Grind veal and trimmings. Put the bones and veal in a large pot and cover with water for 30 minutes. Combine carrots, onions, celery and garlic in a small bowl. Tie bay leaves, parsley and thyme in a cheesecloth. Add vegetables and herbs to pot and cook 4 hours at a medium simmer. Skim, remove herbs and strain. Add salt and pepper and stir until well-mixed. Cool. Freeze for later use. Yields approximately 2 quarts.

THE INN AT LITTLE WASHINGTON
Washington

THE INN AT LITTLE WASHINGTON

For me, experiencing The Inn at Little Washington is akin to looking through a glass prism, watching patterns of light refract to give each ray its own unique splendor.

The exterior, originally a garage in the early 1900s, does not even hint of the interior's elegance.

Once inside, however, the vaulted ceiling designed in a fresco collage reminded me of a Byzantine museum transformed into an exquisite French restaurant. In the main dining room huge, ruffled, peach taffeta lamp shades hang from the ceiling to accent each table set with unusual fresh flowers.

While absorbing the ambiance, my appetizer of Crab and Spinach Timbale was presented under a bell-shaped glass. This delicacy exceeded the expectations my dinner companions, John and Julia Bize, had engendered. Before the entrées, our palettes were exotically cleansed with Fresh Fruit Sorbets.

My entrée of Sweetbreads, sautéed with three mustards and alternating layers of snow peas, was artistically designed to appear as a kaleidoscope. The taste was as fulfilling as its visual appeal. Julia let me sample her Duckling with Shenandoah Apples, an entrée which places duck in an entirely new category. I also snitched a bite of John's succulent Veal Chausseur.

Desserts offered even further visual wonders. I mean, have you ever seen chocolate made to stand up in the shape of a lace fan? Even the Coeur à la Crème was presented in a heart shape and served with a scrumptious Raspberry Sauce.

Co-owners Reinhardt Lynch and Patrick O'Connell behave as if it were effortless. "It's important to appear effortless," said O'Connell. "For instance, one day I was working outside over a brazier when a twister swept the brazier into the sky and scattered chicken over the entire area. Then rain poured, causing a power failure, and dinner had to be cooked by flashlight! We simply added more candles, and the guests never realized our catastrophes."

Compromise simply is not a word in their vocabulary; excellence is, which makes this extraordinary French restaurant a connoisseur's euphoria.

The Inn at Little Washington is located on the corner of Middle and Main streets in Washington. Dinner is served from 6:00 p.m. until 9:30 p.m. on Monday, Wednesday, Thursday and Friday, from 5:30 p.m. until 9:30 p.m. on Saturday and from 4:00 p.m. until 9:30 p.m. on Sunday. For reservations (required) call (703) 675-3800.

THE INN AT LITTLE WASHINGTON'S
CRAB AND SPINACH TIMBALE

Crab Mousse:

½ pound backfin crabmeat
¼ cup heavy cream
1 teaspoon lemon juice
½ teaspoon mustard
½ teaspoon celery salt

dash of cayenne
½ teaspoon salt
½ teaspoon pepper
2 eggs

In a bowl, combine crabmeat, cream, lemon juice, mustard, celery salt, cayenne, salt and pepper. Beat eggs. Blend beaten eggs into crabmeat mixture and refrigerate.

Spinach Timbale:

1 pound fresh spinach
3 tablespoons unsalted
   butter
2 tablespoons flour
¾ cup milk
½ cup heavy cream

1 teaspoon salt
freshly ground pepper to
   taste
⅛ teaspoon grated nutmeg
3 large eggs
pimientos cut into stars

Boil spinach in salted water. Drain, then cool in cold water. Drain and chop finely. Make a roux with butter and flour. Add milk, cream, salt, pepper and nutmeg. Bring mixture to boil. Remove from heat. Stir in spinach. Allow mixture to cool slightly and beat in eggs. Half fill eight buttered molds with crab mousse. Fill remaining half with spinach mixture and place tins in shallow pan of cold water. Bake in

300-degree oven 60 minutes or until set. Cool. Run a knife around edge to unmold. Place on serving plates. Spoon mousse on top and garnish with star-shaped pimiento. Serves 8.

THE INN AT LITTLE WASHINGTON'S
COEUR À LA CRÈME WITH RASPBERRY SAUCE

Filling:

8 ounces cream cheese, softened
⅔ cup sifted confectioners' sugar
1¼ cups heavy cream

1 teaspoon vanilla
1 teaspoon lemon juice
1 teaspoon framboise or kirsch

Using an electric mixer, beat cream cheese until smooth; blend in sugar, a few tablespoons at a time, scraping down sides of bowl. In a chilled bowl, whip cream until stiff. Gently fold half of whipped cream into cream cheese mixture. Add vanilla, lemon juice and framboise, and gently fold in remaining whipped cream. Line either six ½-cup *coeur à la crème* molds, a 3-cup mold with holes or a closely woven basket with a double thickness of dampened cotton cheesecloth. Fill with mixture and cover with cheesecloth and refrigerate overnight. Remove cheesecloth and unmold by inverting onto serving plates. Spoon Raspberry Sauce (recipe below) over each dessert. Garnish with whole berries. Serves 6.

Note: *Coeur à la Crème* molds have tiny holes in the bottom to allow liquids to drain from the cheese.

Raspberry Sauce:

2 pints raspberries (or strawberries), hulled and washed
½ cup sugar

1 tablespoon framboise (raspberry brandy) or kirsch
1 teaspoon lemon juice

Reserve ¼ cup berries for garnish. In blender, purée the remaining berries, sugar, framboise and lemon juice. Strain through a fine sieve.

SKY CHALET COUNTRY INN
Basye

SKY CHALET COUNTRY INN

I magine a chalet nesting in the clouds: a haven so remote that the "frenzies" of this world are powerless to reach you. There is no television set or telephone in your room. You awaken to the aromas of fresh biscuits baking and coffee brewing. You slide from beneath comfy quilts and peer out of your window at the valley.

While your eyes feast on the surrounding Southern Alleghenies to the west or Massanutten Mountain to the east, the smell of those baking biscuits causes you to consider dressing for breakfast. There's no need to be fancy here; a pair of jeans and an old flannel shirt will be fine.

I ambled into the dining room on the cool spring morning to find a fire had already been started in the stone fireplace that reaches to the tip of the cathedral ceiling. Wanting a view of the mountains, I settled down at a table between two couples. One of my neighbors asked if I knew the time, and to my astonishment, I discovered that I had left my watch in the room. Both couples began to laugh with understanding. Forgetting to mark the passage of time is a fairly common occurrence in this relaxing setting.

In the midst of our amusement, the coffee arrived along with the freshly baked biscuits. You could make a whole meal out of the Chalet's biscuits and jellies, but it's wise to leave room for their Potato Pancakes, fresh country Eggs and Sausage.

I had arrived late the night before, so I missed dinner. But my breakfast neighbors launched into full detail. It seems that their Barbecued Beef Ribs, fresh Rainbow Trout and Marinated New York Strip were all prepared in the Chalet's country-gourmet style. Dessert was one of their famous Shenandoah Fruit Crunches.

Mention was also made of the good time had in the Supin Lick Pub, which serves some rather sophisticated cocktails and after-dinner drinks. I toured the rustic lounge, set up with an antique pool table said to be over two hundred years old and the only television set on the premises.

The Sky Chalet is where world-weary congressmen, famous newspeople and exhausted writers go into seclusion. You come here to eat well, sleep well and let the mountain air put your world back into perspective.

Sky Chalet Country Inn is located ten miles from Mt. Jackson, off Route 263 West in Basye. Breakfast is served from 8:30 a.m. until 11:00 a.m. Monday through Friday, and from 8:00 a.m. until 10:00 a.m. on Saturday and Sunday. Lunch is served on weekends only from noon until 2:00 p.m. Dinner is served from 5:00 p.m. until 9:30 p.m. from Wednesday through Sunday. For reservations (recommended on weekends) call (703) 856-2147.

SKY CHALET COUNTRY INN'S
ROAST LOIN OF PORK WITH
SWEET GERMAN SAUERKRAUT

16 ounces sauerkraut
16 ounces apple pie filling
3 to 4 tablespoons brown
  sugar

1 tablespoon caraway seeds
3- to 4-pound pork loin,
  bone removed

Combine sauerkraut, apple pie filling, brown sugar and caraway seeds in the bottom of a roasting pan. Place pork loin in center and spoon mixture over top. Bake in a preheated 350-degree oven until meat thermometer reaches 185 degrees. Serves 6 or more.

SKY CHALET COUNTRY INN'S
BRAISED LAMB SHANKS

¼ cup virgin olive oil
6 lamb shanks or lamb
  chops
salt to taste
1½ teaspoons rosemary

1½ teaspoons garlic powder
1½ teaspoons black pepper
mint jelly

    Heat olive oil in a deep roasting pan on top of stove. If roasting pan is too large for stove, substitute a large skillet and reduce the amount of olive oil. Brown lamb shanks or chops in pan and remove meat. Drain oil and add 1 inch of water to pan. Sprinkle salt and ¼ teaspoon each of rosemary, garlic powder and black pepper on each piece of meat. Put a wire rack in roasting pan just above water. Place meat on rack and cover. Cook at 350 degrees until meat starts to separate from bone. Do not overcook. Serve with mint jelly if desired. Serves 6.

EDINBURG MILL RESTAURANT
Edinburg

EDINBURG MILL RESTAURANT

Would one of today's female teen-agers risk her life for what she believes?

During the Civil War, a teen-ager did just that. General Sheridan's raiders twice set fire to the 1848 Grandstaff Mill in Edinburg because it was supplying flour to Confederate soldiers. Each time, Grandstaff's granddaughters, Nellie and Melvina, persuaded the General to order his soldiers to help townswomen douse the flames. Afterwards, Nellie charmed Sheridan into allowing her to ride his horse. The resourceful girl then sewed a Confederate flag to her petticoats and rode audaciously through the valley warning the Confederacy of Sheridan's plan for attack.

The mill survived, and the charred embers at the front of the building continue to serve as a footnote representing the scars that were left by America's darkest page in history.

Survival is what counts, though, and this old gristmill continued to produce flour for one hundred and thirty years. Then, in 1978, the gears ground to a halt, and a classy country restaurant was established.

The restaurant's interior has retained much of the milling equipment and has been further enhanced by the addition of pierced-tin hanging lanterns. The designer cleverly chose to whitewash some of the original plank walls and adorn them with Edinburg memorabilia. The achieved country-casual look is coordinated with good old-fashioned, country-style recipes. Food is served from a buffet, and salad makings are attractively arrayed in an antique purifier.

My particular loves were the Cheddar Chicken, Stewed Apples and the Sausage Gravy poured over biscuits and corn bread. I knew, after one spoonful, that my husband would love that Sausage Gravy, and I was so right. Their Toll House Pie is an old-fashioned taste delight.

You also can imbibe your favorite cocktail or wine in the Edinburg Mill Lounge, which features entertainment on Friday and Saturday nights. I found that dining in the mill's casual atmosphere provided triple pluses: old fashioned food, relaxation and reminders of our resourceful past.

The Edinburg Mill Restaurant is located on Route 11 on the south edge of town. Meals are served daily. Breakfast is served from 8:00 a.m. until 11:00 a.m. Lunch is served from 11:00 a.m. until 3:00 p.m., but sandwiches are available all day. Dinner is from 3:00 p.m. until 9:00 p.m. Sunday through Thursday, and from 3:00 p.m. until 10:00 p.m. Friday and Saturday. For reservations (required) call (703) 984-8555.

EDINBURG MILL RESTAURANT'S SAUSAGE GRAVY

1 pound mild sausage
4 tablespoons onion, finely
  chopped
2 tablespoons sugar
1 teaspoon salt
½ teaspoon pepper

2 tablespoons
  Worcestershire sauce
¼ cup plain flour
½ cup water
½ cup milk
dash of Kitchen Bouquet

Brown sausage in a skillet, adding one tablespoon at a time to prevent sticking. When sausage is browned, add onions, sugar, salt, pepper and Worcestershire sauce and simmer for two minutes. Add flour, sprinkling evenly on top of sausage. Add water and milk gradually until the right consistency is achieved. Add a dash of Kitchen Bouquet for color. Simmer for 10 to 15 minutes. Serves 6 to 8.

EDINBURG MILL RESTAURANT'S PUMPKIN MUFFINS

1 teaspoon baking soda
⅓ cup water
1 cup pumpkin, cooked
½ cup oil
2 eggs, beaten
1½ cups sugar

1⅔ cups flour, sifted
½ teaspoon baking powder
¼ teaspoon salt
½ teaspoon cinnamon
½ teaspoon nutmeg

Dissolve baking soda in water. Combine all wet ingredients, mixing thoroughly. Sift all dry ingredients together and combine with wet ingredients, stirring until completely blended. Fill non-stick sprayed muffin tins half full. Bake in 350-degree oven until golden brown, about 30 to 35 minutes. Yields 18 muffins.

EDINBURG MILL RESTAURANT'S
CHEDDAR CHICKEN

1 package Cheddar Cheese   **1 stick melted butter**
   Goldfish crackers   **4 chicken breasts**

Coat baking sheet with non-stick cooking spray. Crush crackers in blender and set aside. Melt butter in saucepan. Dip chicken in melted butter and dredge in crushed crackers. Place on baking sheet and bake in 350-degree oven for one hour, uncovered. Serves 4.

WAYSIDE INN
Middletown

WAYSIDE INN
SINCE 1797

If George Washington didn't sleep here, he should have. A majority of the inn's dining rooms honor our first president. Yes, portraits and prints are the expected homages, but displaying the very stump from the cherry tree that little George chopped does lend an unexpected note of whimsey.

In 1797 the inn was opened for bed and board to travelers of the Black Bear Trail. Some twenty years later, the tavern became a stagecoach stop and relay station. Since schedules fluctuated, the tavern keeper sent a young boy to scan the horizon for approaching stagecoaches. As soon as one was spotted, the boy alerted the cook to rekindle the fire so hungry passengers wouldn't have to wait for refreshment.

Somebody must have been on the alert the day I arrived, as I was no sooner seated in the Portrait Room when a steaming bowl of Peanut Soup was set before me. I enjoyed a lot of good peanut soups in my Virginia travels, but noticed that this savory serving leaned more toward a fresh peanut taste than did the others. A crisp green salad accompanied my Chicken Pot Pie. Huge chunks of chicken are enhanced with herbs grown in their garden at the back of the inn. I also found that a splash of a Virginia rosé bestowed a light yet influential touch to my meal.

For dessert I ordered their famous Carrot Cake, and I must say that it lived up to its delectable reputation. Had I really felt the need to put the brakes on those calories, I could have ordered chilled fresh fruit or Prime Rib sans potatoes.

When I return to the Wayside, I'll opt for dining in the Old Slave Kitchen that was discovered, quite by accident, behind a wall only a few years ago. I want to retreat a century or two sitting by that roaring fireplace as I listen to eighteenth-century music played by strolling balladeers.

The more I think about it, George Washington must have dined here. After all, he is credited with being "first in war, first in peace, and first in the hearts of his countrymen." It only makes sense that fine food was another first in his priorities, and this remarkable old inn has always been known for its fine cuisine and hospitality.

The Wayside Inn Since 1797 is located at 7783 Main Street in Middletown. Meals are served daily. Breakfast is served daily from 7:30 a.m. until 11:00 a.m. Lunch is served from 11:30 a.m. until 3:00 p.m., Monday through Saturday. Dinner is served from 5:00 p.m. until 9:00 p.m., Monday through Thursday, and from 5:00 p.m. until 9:30 p.m. on Friday and Saturday. On Sunday, a buffet brunch is served from 11:00 a.m. until 3:00 p.m., with dinner from 3:00 p.m. until 8:00 p.m. For reservations (recommended) call (703) 869-1797.

WAYSIDE INN'S CARROT CAKE

2 cups sugar
4 eggs
1½ cups oil
2 cups self-rising flour
1½ teaspoons baking soda
2 teaspoons cinnamon

2 junior baby food jars of carrots or 2 cups grated carrots
½ cup black walnuts (optional)

Beat sugar, eggs and oil thoroughly and slowly. Add flour, baking soda and cinnamon to first three ingredients, mixing well. Fold in carrots; add nuts (if desired) and mix until well blended. Bake in sheet cake pan at 350 degrees for 40 minutes. Cool. (Can be cooked in angel food cake pan, baking 10 to 15 minutes longer.) Yields 1 cake.

Carrot Cake Icing:
1 stick margarine or butter
8 ounces cream cheese
1 box confectioners' sugar
1 teaspoon vanilla

¼ to ½ cup of coconut (on top)
sprinkle of black walnuts (on top)

Cream margarine and cream cheese together. Add vanilla. Mix in sugar until mixture is smooth. Spread on cake. Add toppings. Garnish with mint leaves and grated carrots to form flower, if desired. Yields 1 cake.

WAYSIDE INN'S ROAST TURKEY
WITH PEANUT DRESSING

1½ cups finely chopped celery
¾ cups finely chopped onion
½ cup fresh snipped parsley
1 cup butter or margarine
2 cups salted peanuts, chopped
1 tablespoon ground sage
1 teaspoon pepper
½ teaspoon salt
12 cups soft bread crumbs
½ cup chicken broth or stock
1 12- to 14-pound turkey cooking oil

In saucepan, sauté celery, onion and parsley in butter or margarine until tender. Stir in peanuts, sage, pepper and salt. Place bread in large mixing bowl and add peanut mixture and chicken broth, mixing well. Rinse turkey; pat dry. Spoon some of the dressing into neck cavity and secure with skewer. Spoon remaining dressing into other cavity; secure and brush turkey breast with cooking oil. Roast (uncovered) in 325-degree oven until meat thermometer registers 185 degrees and drumsticks move easily (about 4½ to 5 hours). Remove and let stand 15 minutes. Serves 24.

WAYSIDE INN'S PRIME RIB

5-pound prime rib
water to cover
2 teaspoons salt
1½ teaspoons pepper
1 teaspoon rosemary
1½ teaspoons sage
1 garlic clove, chopped
1 onion, quartered
1 celery stalk, sliced
1 carrot stick, sliced

Cover prime rib with water. Add vegetables and seasonings and bake in a 350-degree oven for 20 minutes per pound of rib; if a well-done rib is desired, cook longer. Serves 6.

THE RED FOX TAVERN
Middleburg

THE RED FOX TAVERN

George Washington, General Jeb Stuart, Colonel John Mosby, President John F. Kennedy and John Adair have all dined at The Red Fox Tavern. Not familiar with John Adair? Perhaps you've mistakenly heard of him as "Monty," the Confederate Civil War ghost. Recently, Monty made himself so visible to an attractive, mature lady overnighting at the tavern that she snapped his picture. When developed, a parapsychologist and photographer examined the photos and concluded that an entity was indeed captured on film.

Weeks later the lady destroyed the film in an effort to free herself of Monty's presence. Finally, a medium was called who made contact with Monty. The piqued spirit announced that he was John Adair, not Monty, and explained that he had fallen in love with the beautiful woman. The Confederate soldier had traveled home with the lady because, in his time period, it was not safe for a lady to travel alone. The spirit reluctantly agreed to leave when told that the lady was married. So, if staying at the Red Fox, remember their ghost has a penchant for older, attractive women.

Unfortunately, I missed meeting John Adair. Nonetheless, lunching in Joseph Chinn's 1728 ordinary was more than ample compensation. I sat across from the bar allegedly used as an operating table when the tavern functioned as a hospital during the Civil War. Here my taste buds experienced a heavenly Brie in Filo with Pistachio Nut Butter, accompanied by a vibrant Folonara rosé that was perfect with the hearty Red Fox Country Soup. Many of these two-hundred-year-old recipes found their origin here in the nation's foremost area for fox hunting and thoroughbred horse racing. Others, such as the divine Duckling Somerset, are recent adaptations. My meal was concluded with a light, yet tart, Raspberry Champagne Sorbet and a taste of their fantastic homemade Apple Butter Ice Cream.

If you don't intend to burn your calories riding to the hounds, you might choose to lunch on their Watercress and

Endive Salad or a Vegetable Platter. At dinner, the Entrecote (fish broiled in wine) should keep you fit and scrumptiously satisfied.

On my next trip I hope to stay at the Red Fox, sample their Pecan Waffle for breakfast and, who knows, maybe engage John Adair in a friendly tête à tête.

The Red Fox Tavern is located at 2 East Washington Street in Middleburg. Meals are served daily. Breakfast is served daily from 8:00 a.m. until 10:30 a.m. Lunch is served from 11:00 a.m. until 3:00 p.m.; a lightfare menu of soup and salad is served from 3:00 p.m. until 5:00 p.m.; and dinner is from 5:00 p.m. until 9:30 p.m., Monday through Saturday. On Sundays, lunch is served from noon until 3:00 p.m. and dinner from 3:00 p.m. until 8:00 p.m. For reservations (recommended) call (703) 687-6301 in Virginia or toll-free (800) 223-1728 outside Virginia.

THE RED FOX TAVERN'S BRIE IN FILO WITH PISTACHIO NUT BUTTER

filo pastry, 2 leaves
¼ stick clarified butter
Brie, 1 tin

Pistachio Nut Butter (recipe follows)

Lay out filo dough and brush with clarified butter. Place 2 ounces Brie on each filo leaf and add Pistachio Nut Butter over Brie. Fold filo into thirds and seal with clarified butter. Place on greased cookie sheet and put in 450-degree oven until golden brown (a few minutes). Don't overcook. Slice while hot. Serves 3 to 4.

Pistachio Nut Butter:
2 ounces raw pistachios,
shelled and peeled
1 stick unsalted butter

salt and white pepper to
taste

On cookie sheet, roast pistachios at 275 degrees until golden brown. Process in food processor or blender with steel blade until fine. Blend with softened butter. Salt and pepper (white) to taste.

THE RED FOX TAVERN'S RASPBERRY
CHAMPAGNE SORBET

4 pints fresh raspberries or
  5 10-ounce packages of
  frozen
2 cups extra fine sugar,
  divided

1 bottle of champagne
1 whole egg, unshelled, for
  testing
juice of 1 lemon
mint for garnish

If using fresh berries, crush slightly and sprinkle with one cup of sugar and let sit overnight in refrigerator. (Omit marinating overnight if using frozen berries.) The next day drain the juice and discard the pulp. Add the champagne to the raspberry juice and test for sugar density by floating an unshelled egg in the liquid. Continue to add sugar until egg surfaces—at least a half-inch in diameter of the egg should be showing. (When this occurs there is enough sugar.) Remove egg. Add lemon juice and pour mixture into a stainless steel bowl and place in freezer. Stir about once every hour until frozen, or process mixture in ice cream freezer according to machine's directions. Serve garnished with mint. Yields 3 quarts.

KING'S COURT TAVERN
Leesburg

KING'S COURT
TAVERN

When you hear the bell ring at King's Court, it is signaling the opening or closing of the restaurant. A hundred and fifty years ago, when the first proprietor, Mr. Philmore, operated the building as The Country Store, the same bell was used to inform the townspeople of the store's opening and closing. Back in those days much of the store's business was done through bartering; so today, when possible, services are bartered for food and refreshment.

I find that a very appealing way to do business, and in most instances, it's a lot more fun than the monetary transactions most of us are saddled with using.

Arriving at King's Court for a late lunch, I sat at an old wooden table across from a full-service bar. The bar is separated from the dining area, and retains the store's original red oak gingerbread ceiling border. The room is reminiscent of a colonial tavern with the Williamsburg-gray wainscotting that panels the walls. The upper half of the walls are dotted with antique prints, many of which were purchased from Arthur Godfrey's farm. The original, wide windowpanes admit just the right amount of light.

Whenever possible, I prefer to sample a number of items on a restaurant's menu. That way, I can supply more informed suggestions and know which recipes to request. I began with the Potato Soup, made fresh each day, and knew instantly that I wanted to include that recipe for home use. Then I taste-tested their Reuben and Monte Cristo sandwiches, but wound up asking for their London Broil. My recommendation for dessert would have to be the Cheesecake.

The bar offers a large variety of cocktails or a nice selection of wines and beers.

It would be a real treat to return to Leesburg in mid-August when the main streets are blocked off for two days for a colonial celebration. Merrymaking includes clogging, old time music and the display of a variety of colonial crafts.

As a matter of fact, the tin wall sconces at King's Court were fashioned at one of the past summer events. So, mid-August in Leesburg is a good date to put on your calendar when planning a trip through this beautiful countryside.

King's Court Tavern is located at 2 C West Loudoun Street in Leesburg. Lunch is served Monday through Saturday from 11:30 a.m. until 2:00 p.m. Dinner is served from 2:00 p.m. until 9:00 p.m., Sunday through Thursday, and from 2:00 p.m. until 9:30 p.m. Friday and Saturday. The bar is open until 11:00 p.m. Monday through Thursday, and until midnight on Friday and Saturday. Reservations are not accepted, but if you need to call, the phone number is (703) 777-7747.

KING'S COURT TAVERN'S POTATO SOUP *Delicious*

2 tablespoons margarine
2 cups potatoes, peeled and
  chopped
¼ cup fresh parsley,
  chopped
½ cup onion, chopped
1 bay leaf
1 teaspoon salt
1 teaspoon pepper

2½ cups chicken stock or
  broth
2 to 3 cups water
1 cup half and half
3 tablespoons flour
½ cup sour cream
3 to 4 teaspoons chives,
  chopped

Melt margarine in a large pot and sauté potatoes, chopped into cubes, with parsley, onion, bay leaf, salt and pepper. Add chicken stock (or broth) and water, reduce heat to medium and cook for 10 to 12 minutes. Cover and reduce heat to low and cook for 18 to 20 minutes. In a small bowl mix half and half with flour until lumps disappear. Pour into soup, stirring to prevent lumps from forming, and simmer for 30 minutes. Before serving, stir in sour cream and heat through. Sprinkle with chives. Serves 8 to 10.

KING'S COURT TAVERN'S LONDON BROIL

1 1½- to 2-pound flank
  steak
1 cup salad oil
4 tablespoons wine vinegar
¾ teaspoon oregano

¼ teaspoon salt
¼ teaspoon pepper
1 onion, diced
½ pound large mushroom
  caps

Trim flank steak very close, removing all skin, membrane and fat, and place in a large square or rectangular glass dish. Combine salad oil, vinegar, oregano, salt, pepper, onion and mushroom caps and pour over steak. Marinate in refrigerator at least 2 hours or longer. Remove steak from marinade and place on broiler pan. Use pre-heated broiler rack closest to heating unit. Broil for 4 to 5 minutes on each side until meat reaches rare to medium stage. Do not overcook. Remove and slice steak in very thin diagonal slices about ¼-inch thick and serve with Bordelaise Sauce (recipe below). Serves 4.

Bordelaise Sauce:
2 tablespoons butter
1 small onion, chopped
2 shallots
1 cup red wine

1 clove garlic, minced
¼ cup wine vinegar
1 cup brown sauce
chopped parsley

Melt butter in skillet, and sauté onions and shallots until transparent. Combine garlic and vinegar. Add wine and garlic/vinegar mixture. Reduce liquid to half by boiling, and add brown sauce. Serve over meat and garnish with chopped parsley. Yields 1½ cups.

LAUREL BRIGADE INN
Leesburg

LAUREL BRIGADE INN

It is a little-known fact that the Confederate Laurel Brigade, led by Colonel Elijah V. White, never surrendered. When White saw the happenings at Appomattox, he led his troops off to Lynchburg, refusing to take any part of defeat. Prior to Appomattox, the brigade was recognized for gallant conduct, and they signified this distinction with a sprig of laurel in their hatbands. The new name selected for this converted 1766 ordinary is in honor of the brave brigade.

Ellen Flippo Wall told me her father purchased the inn in 1945 because it would have been demolished to make way for a discount store. That was years before preserving the past was championed as an admired undertaking.

The owners worked to preserve the structure's architectural integrity by repairing the combination stone and brick wall that divides the kitchen from the main dining room. The wall was hastily built in 1825 in a special celebration held here for Lafayette, who was visiting President Monroe in nearby Washington.

It was, by all reports, a very festive day. One of the guests became tipsy and disappeared. In the excitement over his absence, the partygoers mistook the mewing of a cat who had fallen into the well for the cries of the missing, tipsy guest. Ah yes, those were spirited times.

The well is still in the inn's beautiful garden, which is governed by a massive osage orange tree. Flowers abound here, including a host of peonies that were planted around 1854. This soothing view made me insist on a table overlooking the garden.

Lunching at Laurel Brigade was like visiting my grandmother. She used to put all the foods cooked during the week on the table at every meal. The food kept reappearing until it was eaten because everyone knows, "It's a sin to waste."

No, they don't serve leftovers. Nevertheless, I wasted not one single bite, remembering how similar their homemade Curried Chicken was to my grandmother's. Their Beef Stew was another good and hearty dish, and the Avocado Mousse made an unusual salad offering. However, I was partial to their Chicken Pot Pie, bountifully laced with hefty chicken chunks.

Apple Brown Betty with Hard Sauce is their dessert specialty, and I was tickled to get that recipe.

Although iced tea suited my mood that day, they do offer a modest selection of wine and alcoholic beverages.

As I was leaving, Mrs. Wall pointed out that the hardware on the front door was installed upside down. So, for the past two hundred and seventeen years it's been necessary to insert the door key in reverse. Just another amusing architectural eccentricity she wouldn't dream of altering.

The Laurel Brigade Inn is located at 20 West Market Street in Leesburg. Lunch is served Tuesday through Saturday from noon until 2:00 p.m. Dinner is from 5:30 p.m. until 8:30 p.m., Tuesday through Thursday, and from 5:30 p.m. until 9:00 p.m. on Friday and Saturday. Sunday dinner is served from noon until 7:00 p.m. For reservations (recommended) call (703) 777-1010.

LAUREL BRIGADE INN'S CURRIED CHICKEN

1 3- to 4-pound stewing
   chicken
1 gallon water
6 tablespoons butter
1 cup onion, finely chopped
1 cup celery, finely chopped
1 cup apple, finely chopped
3 tablespoons flour

1 tablespoon curry powder
2 teaspoons turmeric
2 teaspoons marjoram
salt and pepper to taste
rice (follow package
   directions)
parsley for garnish

Cook the chicken in boiling water until meat separates easily from the bone. Remove the chicken and let liquid reduce. Cube chicken and set aside. In a skillet, melt 3 tablespoons of butter and sauté onions, celery and apple for 7 to 10 minutes. In a saucepan, form a roux with remaining butter and flour. Slowly add about a cup of the reduced chicken liquid to the roux, and stir to combine. Add sautéed vegetables and apples, and season with curry powder, turmeric

115

and marjoram. Salt and pepper to taste. Simmer for 10 minutes. Add the cubed chicken and simmer another 5 minutes. Serve over a bed of parsley-garnished rice. Serves 8.

LAUREL BRIGADE INN'S AVOCADO MOUSSE

1 tablespoon unflavored
  gelatin
2 tablespoons cold water
1 3-ounce package lime
  gelatin

2 cups hot water
1 cup mashed avocado
½ cup mayonnaise
½ cup whipping cream,
  whipped

Dissolve unflavored gelatin in cold water. Dissolve lime gelatin in hot water. Mix gelatins together and chill until slightly thickened. Fold in avocado, mayonnaise and whipped cream. Spoon into 4-cup mold and chill. Serves 6 to 8.

LAUREL BRIGADE INN'S APPLE BROWN BETTY

¼ cup butter
2 cups bread crumbs,
  toasted
4 cups apples, peeled and
  sliced
¼ cup raisins
¼ cup brown sugar

⅛ teaspoon salt
¼ teaspoon nutmeg
1 teaspoon cinnamon
1 tablespoon lemon juice
1 teaspoon vanilla
½ cup apple juice

Melt butter and place in a casserole dish. Add alternate layers of bread crumbs, apples, raisins and brown sugar. Sprinkle with salt, nutmeg and cinnamon. Combine lemon juice, vanilla and apple juice and pour over top. End with a layer of bread crumbs. Bake in a 350-degree oven for 40 minutes. Serve with Hard Sauce (recipe below). Serves 6 to 8.

Hard Sauce:
½ stick margarine
1½ cups confectioners'
  sugar

½ cup apple jack brandy

Place softened margarine, sugar and brandy in blender and blend until smooth. Serve small amount over Apple Brown Betty.

EVANS FARM INN
McLean

EVANS FARM INN

Dreamily sequestered on forty acres of rolling green countryside sits Evans Farm Inn. I first saw this eighteenth-century farm on a day in early spring when my eyes were met with an artist's palette of azaleas and blossoming fruit trees.

True to its farm claim, rows of vegetables and herbs were in their sprouting stages. Seeing a restaurant's growing vegetable garden gives you an idea of what to expect from their food.

As I continued to tour the grounds, I found an old, log smokehouse, a stable turned gift shop and a number of animals for small children to pet.

I then came upon the traditional, old cookhouse where a rather romantic celebration occurred recently. A husband surprised his wife on their eighteenth wedding anniversary by booking a candlelight dinner for the two of them in this quaint old building where their wedding reception had been held.

My tour concluded at the main restaurant, constructed from century-old materials salvaged from churches, mansions and barns. These authentic "oddments," as they are called, lend colonial authenticity to the rooms.

The ingenuity of colonial design is represented in the tremendous antique fireplace, still hung with heavy chains of varying lengths that were used to cook a number of dishes simultaneously.

I sipped a good, old-fashioned Mint Julep in this large, homey main dining room before moving downstairs to have dinner in The Sitting Duck, a casual English pub-styled dining room. The moment I walked through the door, I heard a group crowded around the piano singing *Balling the Jack*.

Luckily, I was able to sample many of the foods that have made Evans Farm Inn famous. It is no surprise that they won the 1985 Fine Dining Hall of Fame award. Served by period-costumed waitresses, my meal began with a unique Onion Soup cooked with paprika-seasoned flour and Provolone cheese. This luscious appetizer was followed by Danish-imported Baby Spareribs, said to be the favorite of Washington Redskins player, Dave Butz. Another inspired sampling is their Seafood Newberg. This dish is usually their buffet staple, owing to its popularity, along with an exceptional Asparagus and Pea Casserole.

For dessert I sampled the super rich Chocolate Cheesecake, the yummy Apple Walnut Cake, made without preservatives, and their esteemed, old Virginia recipe—Apple Crisp.

To enrich my meal, I enjoyed a subtle Riesling while reading a wine list that quotes Plato: "When a man drinks wine at dinner, he begins to feel better pleased with himself." I've noticed that women realize a similar experience; but, in my opinion, a visit to this revitalizing inn is sufficient tonic to put anyone in a better mood.

Evans Farm Inn is located at 1696 Chain Bridge Road in McLean. Lunch is served from 11:30 a.m. until 3:00 p.m., Monday through Saturday; dinner is served from 5:00 p.m. until 9:00 p.m., Monday through Thursday, and 5:00 p.m. until 11:00 p.m. on Friday and Saturday. Brunch is served on Sunday from 11:00 a.m. until 2:00 p.m. Sunday dinner is served from noon until 9:00 p.m. For reservations (recommended), call (703) 356-8000.

EVANS FARM INN'S CHICKEN BARBARA

3 double chicken breasts	1 large onion, sliced
2 cloves garlic	salt and pepper to taste
6 celery stalks, with leaves	dash of rosemary

Place chicken breasts in steamer and add 1 minced garlic clove, 4-inch celery pieces with leaves and onion; steam. When half steamed, season with salt, pepper and rosemary. Steam until cooked, and cool. Remove skin from chicken breasts and cut each chicken breast in half (six pieces in all). Rub each chicken portion with the other cut clove of garlic. Dip chicken in Waffle Batter (recipe below) and fry in deep fat at 375 degrees until golden brown. Serve by placing each chicken portion on top of ¼ cup of Lemon Cream Sauce (recipe below). Garnish with watercress. Serves 6.

Waffle Batter:

1¾ cups sifted flour	½ teaspoon baking soda
1¼ teaspoons baking powder	2 small eggs, separated
	1¼ cups buttermilk

Sift dry ingredients and set aside. Beat egg yolks until frothy. Add buttermilk and beat again. Whip egg whites until stiff. Add flour mixture to buttermilk mixture and beat to a smooth consistency. Fold in egg whites carefully.

Lemon Cream Sauce:

1 tablespoon butter	1 cup light cream or milk
1 tablespoon flour	1 tablespoon lemon juice

In skillet melt butter and add flour, making a roux. Add cream slowly, stirring to incorporate. Add lemon juice and blend until smooth.

EVANS FARM INN'S ASPARAGUS AND PEA CASSEROLE

10½-ounce can of asparagus	½ cup sharp Cheddar cheese, grated
8½-ounce can tiny peas	
8-ounce can water chestnuts	2 tablespoons butter
10¾-ounce can mushroom soup	½ cup bread crumbs, fine

Drain vegetables thoroughly. Slice chestnuts very thin. Grease a casserole dish and place a layer of asparagus, a layer of peas, a layer of water chestnuts, a layer of mushroom soup and a layer of cheese. Repeat layers, ending with cheese on top. Bake in a 325-degree oven 25 to 30 minutes. Melt butter and combine with bread crumbs and spread mixture over top of casserole. Return to oven for 8 to 10 minutes until brown on top. Serves 4.

GADSBY'S TAVERN
Alexandria

GADSBY'S TAVERN

As I stood on the front doorstep of Gadsby's Tavern, I tried to picture how it must have looked to General George Washington, standing there for the last time, reviewing his troops. Even though Alexandria is quaint, you can't deny the intrusion of the twentieth century.

Inside is another story, and if you visit in the evening, it may not be clear which century you've entered. Playing the lute guitar, John Douglas Hall is apt to be singing a Scot song of the eighteenth century, or perhaps interpreting the daily news of the Revolution for the folks who have come to Gadsby's to take their repast.

Built in 1792 by Charles and Ann Mason, Gadsby's four stories were constructed as the City Hotel. In those days, this excellent example of Georgian architecture was considered a veritable skyscraper. The interior was done in such refined taste that no less than six United States presidents have used it for receptions and grand balls. The Blue Ballroom seemed quite small to me, especially when you think that such political notables as George Washington, Marquis de Lafayette, John Paul Jones, John Adams, Thomas Jefferson and James Madison were either doing the minuet or a little "do-si-doing" around this floor during one administration or another.

It is, however, ideal for dining, and patrons today can enjoy many of the same fine foods that our nation's most prominent people loved.

Gadsby's makes their own Sangria and offers other unique alcoholic beverages, including Madeira, a liquid George Washington used for soaking his dentures. I found that a glass of their Sangria is a pleasant way to begin your meal. I ordered the Turkey Devonshire, a rich and creamy open-faced sandwich, and a delicious Clam Chowder for lunch. They also serve their famed Sally Lunn Bread. This is a recipe that was later tested by my mother, who wrote, "I never should have tried this—your father insists that I bake it as a standard food item!"

For a lighter dish, and a good choice in this seaport community, try their Shrimp and Scallops sautéed in a little lemon butter and white wine.

Desserts at Gadsby's are in tune with eighteenth century ingredients, and I chose Washington's favorite, the Buttermilk Pie. It has a satiny-smooth texture and slips down like silk, which makes it difficult to stop at one piece.

Gadsby's is located at 138 North Royal Street in Alexandria. Lunch is served from 11:30 a.m. until 3:00 p.m., Monday through Saturday. Sunday brunch is served from 11:00 a.m. until 3:00 p.m. Dinner is served from 5:30 p.m. until 10:00 p.m., seven nights a week. For reservations (required) call (703) 548-1288.

GADSBY'S TAVERN'S SALLY LUNN BREAD

1 cup milk	⅓ cup sugar
½ cup shortening	½ teaspoon salt
¼ cup water	2 packages active dry yeast
4 cups flour, sifted	3 eggs

Grease two loaf pans. Heat milk, shortening and water to 115 degrees (water should be warm but not hot; shortening need not melt). Blend 1⅓ cups flour, sugar, salt and dry yeast in mixing bowl. Blend warm liquids into flour mix. Beat at medium speed for 2 minutes, scraping sides of bowl. Gradually add ⅔ cup of the remaining flour and the eggs. Beat at high speed for 2 minutes. Add remaining 2 cups of flour and mix (may have to be mixed by hand). Cover, let rise in warm, draft-free place until double in bulk, about 1 hour and 15 minutes. Beat dough down with spatula or at lowest speed with an electric mixer and turn into greased pans. Cover and let rise about 30 minutes in a warm, draft-free place until increased in bulk by one-third to one-half. Bake for 40 to 50 minutes. Yields 2 loaves.

GADSBY'S TAVERN'S BUTTERMILK PIE

2 eggs
2 cups buttermilk
2 cups sugar

8 teaspoons flour
¾ teaspoon lemon extract
1 9-inch deep dish pie crust

In mixing bowl, combine eggs and buttermilk and beat until well mixed. Add sugar and flour gradually, beating until thoroughly incorporated. Add lemon extract and mix only to blend through. Pour into pie crust and bake in 350-degree oven for 30 to 40 minutes. Cool. Yields 1 pie.

GADSBY'S TAVERN'S TURKEY DEVONSHIRE

¾-pound cooked turkey
6 slices bacon
2 tablespoons butter
3 tablespoons flour
1 cup milk

¾ cup Swiss cheese, grated
¼ cup white wine
salt and pepper to taste
4 slices bread, toasted
4 slices tomato

Slice turkey and set aside. In skillet, fry bacon and set aside. In separate skillet, melt butter over medium heat and stir in flour, making a roux. Stir until all lumps are blended into smooth consistency. Add milk and cheese; raise heat and bring to a boil and cook until sauce reaches thick consistency. Remove from heat and stir in wine, salt and pepper. Return to heat and stir until evenly blended. On a baking sheet, place toast and cover evenly with turkey; pour cheese sauce over top. Place a tomato slice and 1½ slices of crumbled bacon over each. Broil for approximately 1 to 2 minutes. Serves 4.

Note: Excellent for leftover turkey.

PORTNER'S
Alexandria

PORTNER'S

At Portner's, the wine is kept in the elevator. Since everyone knows that firemen slide down poles, the elevator at this old fire station was installed during the building's renovation. If your relatives happened by Portner's in 1883, when the building was Columbia County Number Four, they may have joined the town council in chasing hogs off the street to make way for the new steam fire engine. Or, they could have had business on the northern end of Asaph Street with the Robert Portner Brewing Company, which, incidentally, is what the restaurant is named after.

Whatever their venture, I'll bet it was not as gastronomically unique and pleasing as mine. I happened by Portner's just before the lunch hour. Their front window displays a hanging Tiffany stained-glass lamp fashioned into a butterfly. The morning sun's penetration diffused a spray of color through the prisms, causing a captivating effect. Later, I learned that this lamp had been made for the Saint Louis World's Fair and was just one of the many rare antiques comprising Portner's fascinating décor.

The restaurant has four floors with four distinctly dissimilar personalities. Hence, you could dine on separate floors four days in a row and never experience the same atmosphere. From the top floor's Wannamaker Room, done in the Gothic Revival style of the 1870s, you move down a flight to the Burgundy Room, which recreates the Edwardian Period. The main floor bar typifies an early-American saloon, with much of the woodwork made of African mahogany. Descending below ground level is Creighton's Emporium, complete with the actual wall from behind the prescription counter of the 1900 Old Town Drugstore.

Back upstairs in the Saloon I had their highly touted Strawberry Salad, which comes by its fame honestly, followed by a delicious taste of Brunswick Stew. Most of their recipes were found in an antique Virginia cookbook, but I believe their Quesadilla for vegetarians is an adapted creation. With my love for Mexican food, this dish gained high approval.

126

Naturally, their proximity to the ocean provides some marvelous seafood entrées, and my taste of their Backfin Crab Cake knows few parallels. When it comes to desserts, their Very Respectable Hot Fudge Sundae could add some very unrespectable pounds.

If extra poundage is a concern, then stay with their Onion Soup Fondue, a green salad and fresh strawberries for dessert.

Because my taste buds were experiencing a renaissance, I ordered Chateau Saint Michelle, a very smooth wine from Washington state.

Portner's is located at 109 Saint Asaph Street in Alexandria. Meals are served daily. Lunch is from 11:30 a.m. until 6:00 p.m.; dinner is from 6:00 p.m. until 10:30 p.m., Sunday through Thursday, and from 6:00 p.m. until 11:30 p.m. on Friday and Saturday. Sunday brunch is from 10:30 a.m. until 3:00 p.m. For reservations (recommended) call (703) 683-1776.

PORTNER'S STRAWBERRY SALAD

1 pint strawberries	ground black pepper
3 to 4 cucumbers	sprinkles of sugar
cabbage or Chinese celery	

Vinaigrette:

2 cups warm water	½ teaspoon salt
2 cups white vinegar	½ tablespoon coarsely
¾ cup sugar	ground pepper

Wash, destem and slice ripe strawberries in half and refrigerate. Peel cucumbers, slice lengthwise and scoop out seeds. Slice cucumbers ¼-inch thick in the shape of half moons. Combine ingredients for vinaigrette and marinate cucumbers for two hours in refrigerator.

To assemble salad, line chilled plates with the inner, tender leaves of cabbage or Chinese celery. Place a spoonful of marinated cucumbers on top of the cabbage leaves, and top with strawberries. Sprinkle additional cucumbers vinaigrette over berries. Top with freshly ground black pepper and a sprinkle of sugar. Serves 4 to 6.

PORTNER'S QUESADILLA

4 10-inch stone ground flour tortillas

1 cup grated Monterey Jack cheese

1 cup grated Colby cheese

2 ripe avocados

1 4¼-ounce can chili peppers, whole

1 cup Salsa Cilentro (recipe follows)

2 teaspoons crushed red peppers

3 tablespoons clarified butter or vegetable oil

2 ounces sour cream

Sprinkle tortillas evenly with both cheeses. Slice avocados thinly, and place slices over cheeses. Halve chili peppers; place over avocados. Spread salsa over peppers (reserving 4 teaspoons or so for garnish). Sprinkle with crushed red peppers. (Tortillas can be made ahead and refrigerated until needed.)

Pour clarified butter or oil into two 12-inch sauté pans (prepare tortillas one at a time). Cook tortillas over moderate heat until the cheese begins to melt and the bottom of the tortilla is lightly browned. Remove from pans and fold tortillas in half and place in casserole dish. Can be kept in 140-degree oven up to 45 minutes. Before serving, spoon sour cream and the extra salsa over tortillas. Serves 4.

Salsa Cilentro:

6 tomatoes, cored

2 to 3 fresh jalapeño peppers, cored

2 medium red onions, minced

1 teaspoon cumin

1 bunch fresh cilentro, stemmed (or 1 to 2 teaspoons of dried cilentro)

1½ teaspoons sugar

¾ teaspoon salt

Coarsely chop tomatoes and jalapeños and set aside. In food processor or blender, process remaining ingredients until mixture resembles a fine relish. Mix all ingredients together and store in tightly covered container in refrigerator until needed. Will keep for several days. Serves 4.

MOUNT VERNON INN
Mount Vernon

MOUNT VERNON INN

The fifteen miles on the Mount Vernon Memorial Highway from our nation's capital to George Washington's estate at Mount Vernon comprise one of the most scenic drives in the United States. It wasn't so idyllic in Washington's day. The roads to Mount Vernon back then were poor under the best of conditions and all but impassable during bad weather. With the approach of the two hundredth anniversary of Washington's birthday, Congress allotted $7.2 million for the construction of the memorial highway. Completed in time for the celebration in 1932, it survives as a tribute to our first president and the man who led the Continental Army during the American Revolution.

Meals were served to the public at Mount Vernon as far back as 1872, when Colonel James Hollingsworth ran a small operation out of the estate's kitchen. When the memorial highway was constructed, a new concessions building owned by the National Park Service was erected just off the grounds of the estate. In 1981, the Mount Vernon Ladies' Association of the Union purchased the rights to operate the concession and named it the Mount Vernon Inn.

Visitors to the inn are greeted by service staff in Colonial costumes. In wintertime, three functioning fireplaces among the five different dining rooms help keep guests comfortable. If you're lucky enough to be seated in the Potomac Room, you'll immediately notice the 360-degree mural depicting Mount Vernon during Colonial days. It was painted by nationally renowned artist Virginia McLaughlin of Gettysburg, Pennsylvania. A smaller mural in the lobby presents a view of the west side of the manor house.

The inn serves traditional American cuisine, with the accent on fresh seafood and game and hand-carved beef. Fresh herbs and edible flowers grown on the Mount Vernon estate complement dinner entrées. Several Virginia wines are available by the glass or bottle. The Roasted Pheasant Stuffed with Apples, Walnuts and Figs is a big favorite around

130

Christmastime. For dessert, be sure to try the Homemade Colonial Bread Pudding, one of the inn's classics.

Mount Vernon Inn offers the best of our country's early days, with authentic costumes and décor and food that would please any president from George Washington onward. Amid the comfortable surroundings, it's funny how even sticklers for historical accuracy don't seem to miss the well-worn roads traveled by the father of our country.

Mount Vernon Inn is located outside the front gate of the Mount Vernon Plantation, south of Alexandria. Lunch is served from 11:00 a.m. until 3:30 p.m. seven days a week. Dinner is served from 5:00 p.m. until 9:00 p.m. Monday through Saturday. For reservations (recommended for dinner) call (703) 780-0011.

MOUNT VERNON INN'S BAKED OYSTERS SCARBROUGH

32 fresh large oysters
1/2 pound lean bacon
3 cloves garlic, finely minced
1/4 cup all-purpose flour
1/4 cup melted butter
1 quart half-and-half
1 tablespoon cayenne pepper
1 tablespoon white pepper
1 tablespoon oregano
1/2 cup chopped fresh parsley
1 1/2 cups breadcrumbs
1/2 cup dry sherry
1 cup grated Parmesan cheese
1 cup sour cream

Shuck oysters and put them on the half shell. Reserve in refrigerator. Preheat oven to 400 degrees. Fry bacon and add garlic, removing from heat immediately when garlic turns nutty yellow. Place flour in a large mixing bowl and blend in bacon mixture and remaining ingredients, adding sour cream at the end. Mixture should form a thick paste. Cover oysters with approximately 1 tablespoon of the paste each and bake 10 to 15 minutes until golden brown. Serves 8.

131

MOUNT VERNON INN'S HOMEMADE COLONIAL BREAD PUDDING

2 cups dry breadcrumbs
4 cups half-and-half
1 cup sugar
$^1/_2$ tablespoon butter
$^1/_4$ teaspoon salt

$^1/_4$ teaspoon nutmeg
$^1/_2$ teaspoon cinnamon
5 eggs, lightly beaten
2 teaspoons vanilla
$^1/_2$ cup raisins

Soak breadcrumbs in half-and-half for six minutes. Add sugar, butter, salt, nutmeg and cinnamon. Pour slowly over eggs. Add vanilla and raisins. Mix well, then pour into buttered 9-inch by 12-inch baking dish. Bake in pan of hot water at 350 degrees for 1 hour. Serves 6 to 8.

MOUNT VERNON INN'S ROASTED PHEASANT STUFFED WITH APPLES, WALNUTS AND FIGS

4 Granny Smith apples,
    peeled, cored and diced
12 dried Mission figs, diced
1 cup chutney
$^1/_2$ cup chopped walnuts

$^1/_2$ cup breadcrumbs
1 tablespoon allspice
pinch of salt
4 pheasants

Preheat oven to 400 degrees. Blend apples, figs, chutney, walnuts, breadcrumbs, allspice and salt, then stuff cavities with mixture. Truss the legs together. Pull string around bodies, then tie wings together. Place on rack in roasting pan large enough to hold all pheasants. Roast for 20 minutes. Reduce temperature to 350 degrees and continue roasting for 1 hour and 15 minutes. Serves 8.

KENMORE INN
Fredericksburg

KENMORE INN

As my daughter and I walked up the path to the Kenmore Inn, its grand image set the scene for the soft, understated atmosphere of luxury that characterizes the inn's interior.

Although the inn, built as a private home in the late 1700s, has changed its status a number of times in the intervening years, we were lucky to discover it just one week after it had been completely renovated.

The renovators were very careful to maintain the fancy "egg and ball" carved woodwork used in the archways, which gives the inn a unique blend of English and old Fredericksburg elegance.

The very wide, ornate foyer leads through rich burgundy carpeting into the bar, done in navy blue with occasional petit point chairs, or the main dining room, decorated in gray and pink pastels.

The main dining room was our selection for lunch. Our table was set with a pink linen tablecloth and wine-colored napkins. Fresh pink carnations with a sprig of lavender adorned our table.

A light salad garnished with fresh sprouts and the restaurant's own blend of hot tea began our meal. As recommended, I had their Broccoli Quiche, which is a tasty dish, but I also took some bites of my daughter Daintry's Spinach Salad, served with a piquant dressing.

For dessert we taste-tested their Almond Custard Cake, which we liked so much that we finished the entire slice. We were not interested in alcoholic beverages at lunch, but the inn does offer quite a nice selection.

The next time we visit Fredericksburg, it would be fun to stay in this posh inn and have dinner here, as well as lunch.

The Kenmore Inn is located at 1200 Princess Anne Street in Fredericksburg. Lunch is served daily from 11:30 a.m. until 2:30 p.m., and dinner from 5:30 p.m. until 9:30 p.m. Tuesday through Sunday. For reservations (recommended) call (703) 371-7622.

KENMORE INN'S RICH CREAM SCONES

1 cup plus 2 tablespoons
  plain flour
1 tablespoon baking
  powder

pinch of salt
4 to 5 tablespoons butter
¼ cup sour cream
1 egg

Sift flour and baking powder in bowl. Add salt, rub in butter lightly with fingertips. With a spoon make a deep hollow impression and pour in sour cream and well-beaten egg. Make into soft dough, turn onto floured board. Roll out lightly to ½-inch thickness. Cut into rounds, place on greased cookie sheet. Prick rounds with fork. Bake 10 to 12 minutes in 375-degree oven until golden. Serve with any jam or jelly. Yields 10 to 12.

KENMORE INN'S EYEMOUTH TART

8 ounces Pie Crust Pastry
  (see Index)
6 tablespoons sugar
2 ounces walnuts
2 ounces currants
2 ounces coconut, shredded

2 ounces cherries
2 ounces raisins
1 egg, beaten
2 tablespoons butter, melted
1 cup confectioners sugar
cold water

Roll out pastry and line 12-inch by 14-inch pan. Mix all dry ingredients, except confectioners' sugar. Add egg and melted butter and combine mixture. Spread mixture over pastry and bake in 375-degree oven until golden—about 30 minutes. Mix confectioners sugar with enough cold water for spreading consistency. Ice while still hot. Yields 16.

KENMORE INN'S CUCUMBER CREAM FLAN

Pastry Dough:

5 ounces flour
dash of salt
6 tablespoons butter, cut in
  lumps

3 to 4 tablespoons iced
water

In mixing bowl combine flour and salt; cut in butter lumps until grainy. Add iced water and press against bowl until it forms a mass. Remove and roll out on floured board and place in 7½-inch flan tin or 8-inch pie plate.

Flan:

2 cucumbers, sliced
4 ounces cream cheese
3 tablespoons mayonnaise
2 tablespoons chopped
  chives

salt and pepper to taste
cucumber slices for garnish

Finely chop cucumbers, except for garnish slices. Work cream cheese and mayonnaise in bowl until blended. Fold in cucumbers and chives. Salt and pepper to taste. Fill flan tin with mixture and level off with knife. Bake at 350 degrees about 25 to 30 minutes, until flan puffs up. Serves 6.

LA PETITE AUBERGE
Fredericksburg

LA PETITE AUBERGE The ladies who crossed the street in 1880 to prevent being seen walking past McCracken's, a liquor store with a questionable reputation, would be the first to walk through the door today.

A posh establishment known as La Petite Auberge has moved into this old store that has turned from liquor to hardware to excellent French cuisine.

The interior is really a surprise. Instead of a dark décor and the classical sounds of Vivaldi, it appears as a French sidewalk café, and the accompaniment is light, contemporary music. White latticed fences line exposed brick walls attractively decorated with paintings evocative of the French Impressionists. Tables are set with white linen, candles and fresh flowers.

After a day of traveling, a Strawberry Daiquiri was most tantalizing.

All the appetizers looked interesting, but since I had never tasted Asperges Ravigotte, I thought this was a good time. The presentation, which always adds so much to the enjoyment of a dish, was especially attractive. Strawberries and asparagus were cut into petals to form the shape of an unfolding flower.

My daughter, Daintry, was impressed, but pointed out that her Vichyssoise, garnished with strawberry slivers, was also something special.

I had been told by friends that I hadn't tasted Soft-shelled Crab until I'd tasted those at the Auberge. Prepared in an understated French sauce and garnished with almonds, this delicacy comes awfully close to a divine creation in my repertoire of food tasting. I decided on a 1975 Chateau La Gravette Bordeau to complement my seafood.

Daintry, who had Tornedoes au Poivre Vert, a beef tenderloin sautéed with green peppercorns, kept nudging me to get that recipe. But you can't get them all, and after trying their Sausage Provencal, I knew my husband would love that one. And he did.

138

For dessert, Daintry "pigged out" on their Grand Marnier Cake, while I sipped a French brandy.

The Auberge is a restaurant for any occasion.

La Petite Auberge is located at 311 William Street in Fredericksburg. Lunch is served from 11:30 a.m. until 2:30 p.m., Monday through Friday. Dinner is served from 5:30 p.m. until 10:00 p.m., Monday through Saturday. For reservations (required) call (703) 371-2727.

LA PETITE AUBERGE'S BACK FIN CRAB NORFOLK

5 tablespoons butter
1 teaspoon shallots,
  chopped
5 drops Tabasco sauce
1½ tablespoons capers
¼ teaspoon Old Bay
  Seasoning

1 pound back fin crabmeat
8 to 10 boiled new potatoes
lemon wedges
parsley for garnish

Melt butter to the foam stage, add shallots, Tabasco, capers and Old Bay Seasoning and cook until shallots are tender. Add crabmeat, swirl in skillet a few times, reduce heat to medium, cover and cook about 4 minutes. Serve with potatoes and garnish with lemon wedge and parsley. Serves 4.

LA PETITE AUBERGE'S SOFT-SHELLED CRABS

8 small soft-shelled crabs,
  cleaned
flour for dredging
4 tablespoons butter

salt and pepper to taste
2 ounces toasted almonds
2 shallots, chopped
1 lemon

Preheat oven to 450 degrees. Dredge soft-shelled crabs in flour. Using 2 skillets, melt 2 tablespoons of butter in each. Place 4 crabs in each skillet, back side down, for 2 to 3 minutes; turn over for 1 to 2 minutes. Salt and pepper to taste. Place both skillets in oven for 4 to 5 minutes with almonds, shallots and a squeeze of lemon juice over each. Serves 4.

LA PETITE AUBERGE'S SAUSAGE PROVENCAL

2 pounds rope sausage
  (mild Italian)
2 green peppers, coarsely
  cut
1 red pepper, coarsely cut
3 small tomatoes, chopped
4 cloves garlic, crushed
½ teaspoon rosemary
½ teaspoon thyme
2 bay leaves
dash of crushed red pepper
¼ teaspoon fennel seeds
1 teaspoon cornstarch
1 cup dry white wine
fettucine (follow package
  directions)

Cut sausage into 12 equal portions. In mixing bowl, combine peppers, tomatoes, garlic, rosemary, thyme, bay leaves, crushed red pepper, fennel and cornstarch and stir until well mixed. Put mixture in bottom of large frying pan, placing sausage on top. Add wine and cook on top of stove until mixture reaches a boil; boil for about 3 minutes. Remove and bake in 425-degree oven, covered, for 25 to 30 minutes. Remove and serve with prepared fettucine. Serves 6 to 8.

OLDE MUDD TAVERN
Thornburg

OLDE MUDD TAVERN

Legend purports that six brothers named Mudd left Bethnal Green, England, for America in 1665. Three of the brothers (one of whom was a forebearer of the famous Dr. Sam Mudd, who treated John Wilkes Booth) settled in Maryland. The remaining three went to Virginia, and it was brother James who supposedly started an oxcart stop in Thornburg. As the local population increased, the business branched out to become a tavern. The original wood and mud structure was burned during the Civil War but was soon rebuilt in fieldstone with six white dormers across the front.

The government had the tavern, which was located in front of the house, torn down in 1917 to make way for a junction. Later, in 1979, the Vitarius family turned the house into one of Virginia's most superb restaurants. As I entered the pre-Civil War home, the classical baroque sounds of a harpsichord, played in the foyer, began to push back the years for me.

I dined in the General Lee Room beneath Lee's portrait. Spring was in strong evidence at my table, appealingly set with a bouquet of irises and azaleas atop a linen tablecloth.

I realized this was going to be a one-of-a-kind feast when no less than five different freshly baked hot breads were served with apple butter. These gastronomical pleasures were followed by a relish tray and a wine list printed on a silver-colored fan.

A white chardonnay seemed an appropriate selection to enhance their Clam Appetizer and Deviled Crab Entrée. Both dishes are worth at least four stars, but their vegetables tip the five-star category. Zucchini in Tomato Sauce, Hawaiian Carrots, Creamed Spinach and Bourbon Sweet Potatoes are a ticket to culinary fame for owner and chef Vitarius.

Believe it or not, room was found for their Almond Cheesecake, which deserves not a star less than the other dishes.

Vitarius is equally creative in preparing dishes that won't ruin your calorie count. Prime Rib or Broiled Sirloin with a green salad should help you retain your status quo.

142

Wandering through the other dining rooms, also named for Southern generals, it was obvious that the sentiment remains in the South, but the cuisine belongs to no particular region. This restaurant is a true traveler's "find," which I intend to find again on my next trip.

The Olde Mudd Tavern is located on U.S. 1 and Route 606 in Thornburg. Dinner is served from 4:00 p.m. until 9:00 p.m., Wednesday through Saturday, and from noon until 9:00 p.m. on Sunday. The tavern is closed during the first week in February and the first week in July, as well as on December 24 and 25 and January 1. For reservations (recommended) call (703) 582-5250.

OLDE MUDD TAVERN'S
BOURBON SWEET POTATOES

½ pound brown sugar
1 46-ounce can of apple
  juice
2 cinnamon sticks
1 cup dark corn syrup

2 tablespoons cornstarch
½ cup water
1 ounce bourbon
1 pound sweet potatoes,
  boiled

In saucepan combine sugar, apple juice, cinnamon sticks and corn syrup over medium heat. Lower to simmer and cook one hour or more. Combine cornstarch with water and add to thicken mixture. Add bourbon, stirring to combine. Add boiled sweet potatoes and cook 20 minutes. Serves 4 to 6.

OLDE MUDD TAVERN'S ZUCCHINI
IN TOMATO SAUCE

Sauce:
1 small onion, chopped
2 stalks celery, chopped
½ of green pepper, chopped
½ cup fresh mushrooms,
  sliced
2 tablespoons oil

pinch of parsley
¼ teaspoon oregano
½ teaspoon garlic salt
pinch of sweet basil
1 16-ounce can of tomatoes
3 ounces tomato paste

143

In skillet, sauté vegetables in oil; add spices, tomatoes and tomato paste. Simmer for 1 hour.

Zucchini:

2 large zucchini	salt to taste
3 tablespoons oil	pinch of oregano
2 grinds of black pepper	

Wash zucchini and rub down to smooth edges on peeling. Slice diagonally. In skillet, sauté in oil adding pepper, salt and oregano. Simmer until half-cooked and add sauce, cooking for 20 minutes. Serves 4 to 6.

OLDE MUDD TAVERN'S CREAMED SPINACH

Sauce:

6 to 8 bacon strips	3 cups chicken stock
1 small onion, chopped	pinch of nutmeg
1 to 2 teaspoons oil	salt and pepper to taste
2 tablespoons flour	2 tablespoons sour cream

Fry bacon and set aside. Sauté onion in bacon drippings and drain grease. Add oil and flour, stirring to make a roux. Add chicken stock, stirring with whisk until slightly thickened to light sauce. Cook on medium-low heat about 30 minutes. Stir in nutmeg, and salt and pepper to taste. Add sour cream and heat through.

Spinach:

1 pound spinach	grind of black pepper
2 tablespoons clarified butter	salt to taste
	2 ounces anisette

Wash spinach well and remove stems. Dip spinach in boiling water until it wilts. Remove, drain, and set aside to cool. In skillet, add butter and cooled spinach; add a grind of pepper and salt, sautéing for 5 minutes. Add anisette and simmer 5 minutes. Add sauce and simmer until flavors blend for 20 to 30 minutes. Serves 4 to 6.

HANOVER TAVERN
Hanover

HANOVER TAVERN

Few people know that, while earning his law degree, Patrick Henry tended bar (often barefoot) at Hanover Tavern. His alternative occupation was the result of marriage to Sarah, the daughter of tavern owner John Shelton. The young couple lived at the tavern that was originally built as a stagecoach stop in 1723. And, it was from the tavern that Henry was called across the street to the courthouse in 1763 to fight for the farmers against King George III. Henry's case, ironically known as the Parsons' Cause, was actually anti-parsons. Henry proved that parsons were the guilty middlemen in a royal tax "rip-off" of the colonial farmers.

History had yet other episodes to record at the Hanover, and some eighteen years later, word came to the tavern that Cornwallis and Tarleton were approaching. Remember those old western movies in which everyone ran out of the saloon and jumped on the first available horse? It is said that when the British were sighted, the exit was so hasty that it took a week before all the horses were returned to their rightful owners. During this confusion, Cornwallis requisitioned the tavern and made it his headquarters for eighteen days, and then left—neglecting to pay his bill.

The bill of fare in these colonial dining rooms varies with each theatrical production at the adjacent Barksdale Theatre. The night of our visit we enjoyed Ham Biscuits, their famous Stewed Apples, Shrimp Salad and Cheese Corn—all washed down with a light rosé wine. The custard-type cake looked very appetizing, but my calorie counter told me that I'd better substitute the play for dessert. And what a dessert it was. *A Coupla White Chicks Sitting Around Talking* surely aided my calorie reduction because I expended so much energy laughing!

It's good entertainment, which is what this oldest dinner theater in America is famous for. The repertoire includes everything from *Antigone* to musicals, with a sprinkling of light opera. The Barksdale Theatre group, which began renovating this tavern in 1953, has converted it into a living historical landmark. However, this establishment goes one step beyond by serving both delicious food and great theater. An unbeatable combination!

Hanover Tavern and Barksdale Theatre are located on Highway 301 in Hanover. Cocktails are served from 6:00 p.m.; dinner is served from 7:00 p.m. until 8:30 p.m., Wednesday through Saturday. Year-round performances, given Wednesday through Saturday, begin at 8:30 p.m. For reservations (required) call (804) 537-5333.

HANOVER TAVERN'S STEWED APPLES

2 cups apples, cooked and
   mashed
½ cup brown sugar
4 tablespoons cornstarch
1 teaspoon cinnamon

½ teaspoon nutmeg
1 teaspoon vanilla
1 teaspoon lemon juice
½ teaspoon salt
3 tablespoons butter

Place apples in medium-size bowl; mix sugar and cornstarch and add to apples, mixing well. Add remaining ingredients, except butter, and mix thoroughly. Pour mixture into an 8-inch square, greased baking dish and dot with butter. Bake in 350-degree oven for 30 to 45 minutes. Serves 6.

HANOVER TAVERN'S SHRIMP SALAD

1 pound tiny shrimp,
   shelled and boiled
1 pound macaroni, cooked
½ cup grated cabbage
⅓ cup mayonnaise
⅓ cup pickle relish

1½ tablespoons mustard
1 teaspoon celery seed
1 celery stalk, diced
2 tablespoons onion, grated
1 egg, hard boiled, chopped

In large mixing bowl, combine all ingredients using mayonnaise to bind. May add more mayonnaise if necessary. Chill. Serves 8 to 10.

147

HANOVER TAVERN'S CHEESE CORN

1 16-ounce can of corn
5 tablespoons grated sharp
  Cheddar cheese
½ of small green pepper,
  chopped

½ of small onion, chopped
salt and pepper to taste
¾ stick butter
2 pieces cubed bread,
  toasted

In mixing bowl, place drained corn, cheese, green pepper, onion, salt and pepper, mixing well. In saucepan, melt butter and add cubed toast or bread crumbs. Pour corn mixture into an 8-inch, greased baking dish, and cover with butter and bread crumb mixture. Bake in 350-degree oven about 30 minutes or until golden brown. Serves 4.

FOX HEAD INN
Manakin-Sabot

FOX HEAD INN

The TV cameras were rolling, and the director shouted, "Action!" Then the stuntman for popular daytime soap *Search For Tomorrow* walked forward as, on cue, the car spun in the Fox Head Inn's driveway, "hit" its intended victim, and sped away from the scene of the crime.

On the soap, the inn is called The Hartford House. Fox Head was chosen for filming because its pastoral beauty and authentic nineteenth-century architectural charm produced just the right setting.

Fox Head's manager, Scott Pettit, made what he called his television debut and exit when he held an IV over the actor who was supposedly being rushed to the hospital.

Scott's mother, Barbara Pettit, told me they hadn't had so much excitement in this tucked-away corner of historic Goochland County since the evening an avalanche of secret service men tumbled out of two black limousines. They had come to check the security for a Saudi Arabian sheik. The sheik was visiting the area to study a local hospital and was advised, excellently so, to dine at the Fox Head.

The restaurant is described as a farmhouse. It was built at the turn of the century by Mr. Raleigh Mills. It's been said that Mills had to raise the original one-story roof with railroad jacks in order to provide additional room for his seven children. Perhaps it's the height that gives the structure a more elegant appearance than the usual farmhouse.

Inside, the four dining rooms depict past and present regional interests. The Hunt Room conveys the restaurant's name and is decorated in the pinks of fox hunters. It features an unusual horseshoe-shaped table and various hunting paraphernalia. The Country Kitchen is adorned with old bottles and the now rare, blue graniteware. The Thoroughbred Room displays not only the pictures of winning horses from local stables but also miniature jockey figurines, mounted on wall brackets, wearing their stables' colors.

It would be difficult to choose a favorite, but I am partial to the Tobacco Room. My daughter, Daintry, and I dined in this nostalgic room that sports a gigantic old Bull Durham poster, the type I used to see on highway billboards when I was a child.

Daintry was especially pleased with their Seafood Casserole—a combination of shrimp and lobster in a sherry-cream sauce. I decided on the Scampi, cooked with Dijon mustard and lemon juice in a white wine sauce. The beauty of this dish is it doesn't taste low-cal, but it is!

The Fox Head's cuisine, which also includes steaks and fried chicken, was described in *Victorian Magazine* as "neither haute cuisine, nor city slick, nor country." It is, however, excellent, with especially creative touches given to vegetables, in particular the Cymling (squash) Cakes, and desserts.

Two of their real standout desserts are the Fox Hunter Pie, served with a bourbon-laced, whipped cream topping, and their homemade Creme de Menthe Ice Cream.

The Midori cocktails we imbibed before dinner and the Virginia wine ordered with dinner helped make dining at the Fox Head a relaxing and memorable experience.

The Fox Head Inn is located on Route 621 in Manakin-Sabot. Dinner is served Monday through Saturday from 6:30 p.m. until 8:00 p.m. For reservations (required) call (804) 784-5126.

FOX HEAD INN'S CYMLING CAKES

1 large cymling (squash)
1 medium Vidalia onion, grated
1 egg, beaten
½ teaspoon salt
1 tablespoon sugar
1 cup flour
1½ teaspoons baking powder
¼ teaspoon pepper
oil for frying

151

Grate squash, using coarse side of grater. In medium-sized mixing bowl, place grated cymling and grated onions, and add all ingredients except oil. Mix until thoroughly incorporated. Shape mixture into 8 patties. Pour about 2 tablespoons of oil into skillet and fry patties on both sides over medium-high heat until cooked through the centers. Serves 4.

FOX HEAD INN'S BLUE CHEESE DRESSING

1 pint mayonnaise
¾ cup buttermilk
¼ teaspoon garlic powder
½ teaspoon Worcestershire
  sauce
2 tablespoons crushed
  pineapple
2 ounces blue cheese,
  crumbled

In blender or mixing bowl, add mayonnaise and buttermilk and blend until mixed. Add garlic powder, Worcestershire sauce and crushed pineapple and mix until smooth. Add blue cheese and mix only until combined. Pour in container with tight fitting lid and store in refrigerator. Yields over 3 cups.

LEMAIRE RESTAURANT
Richmond

LEMAIRE RESTAURANT

Atmosphere can influence your mood. If an atmosphere gives you the feeling that you are in a palace, then your manner changes to accommodate that perception. From the moment that I entered the Palm Court at the magnificently renovated Jefferson Hotel, built in 1895, I knew I was in for a regal treat. A marble statue of Thomas Jefferson, bathed in beams of colored lights from the overhead stained-glass dome, greeted me. Originally, the room featured a pool of live alligators, but they became a source of concern when one day a six-foot specimen was found under a desk in the reading room. A woman, writing at the desk, put her feet on a convenient footstool only to have the stool suddenly move. The renovators have wisely substituted alligators of brass.

Connecting the Palm Court and the Rotunda is a grand staircase resembling the Pompeian style. From the mezzanine of the amazing two-and-a-half-story Rotunda, I watched guests mingle while music from a grand piano filled the room with its faux marble columns. By this time, I knew that I was in the presence of grandeur.

Could the food from their main restaurant, Lemaire, possibly live up to this atmosphere? I was skeptical. The restaurant is named for Jefferson's French maître d'hotel, Etienne Lemaire, who introduced the art of cooking with wine to America. Instead of a single, large room, Lemaire is a series of seven rooms, one featuring a library with part of the original collection of Jefferson's books. I dined there in a private alcove.

As soon as I was seated, I was given delicious, complimentary deep-fried artichokes served with a piquant horseradish sauce. Because I had arrived in the late afternoon, I wasn't interested in a full dinner, so I sampled their hearty Black Bean Soup with Smithfield Ham and Sherry. From their international wine list I chose the Château Olivier–Graves Bordeaux, which was the right complement to their Oysters à la Jefferson. The scrumptious oysters served on grilled corn

154

bread and smothered with a light lemon hollandaise are a true Southern appetizer with a continental twist. In fact, that description captures Lemaire's entire cuisine—regional food enhanced by international technique.

I sampled their ultrarich Black Velvet Chocolate Mousse, which should keep chocoholics satisfied for a day or so, but my favorite was their Chocolate Chip Charlotte, which lends a sensation of three different tastes and shouldn't be missed.

Lemaire Restaurant is located in the Jefferson Sheraton Hotel at Franklin and Adams streets in Richmond. Breakfast is served daily from 6:30 a.m. until 11:00 a.m.; lunch is served from noon until 3:00 p.m.; and dinner is served from 5:30 p.m. until 10:00 p.m. For reservations, call (804) 788-8000, extension 1139.

LEMAIRE'S BLACK BEAN SOUP
WITH SMITHFIELD HAM AND SHERRY

1 pound black beans	4 bay leaves
2 tablespoons bacon fat	salt
2 medium onions, diced	ground white pepper
1/2 cup diced carrots	2 ounces dry sherry
1/2 cup diced celery	3 tablespoons sour cream
1/8 teaspoon minced garlic	4 ounces Smithfield ham,
3 quarts chicken stock	julienned
2 smoked ham hocks	

Rinse beans and soak them overnight in a quart of water. Heat bacon fat in a skillet and sauté onions, carrots, celery and garlic until onions are clear but not brown. Place chicken stock in a pot and add beans, ham hocks, bay leaves and salt and white pepper to taste. Cover and bring to a boil. Lower heat to simmer and cook until beans are soft. Add sautéed vegetables to beans and cook slowly uncovered for at least 1 hour. Discard bay leaves and puree half of the bean mixture. Return the puree to the soup. Serve with sherry and garnish with a dollop of sour cream and equal portions of Smithfield ham. Serves 10 to 12.

LEMAIRE'S OYSTERS A LA JEFFERSON

Corn Cakes:

1½ cups buttermilk   ½ cup all-purpose flour
1 egg, slightly beaten   ½ teaspoon salt
2 tablespoons bacon fat or   1 teaspoon baking powder
    butter, melted   1 teaspoon sugar
1 cup corn meal

Place a greased 12-inch by 8-inch by 2-inch baking pan in oven. Preheat oven to 425 degrees. In a mixing bowl, combine buttermilk, egg and bacon fat or butter and mix until blended. In a separate bowl, sift together corn meal, flour, salt, baking powder and sugar and add to buttermilk mixture. Beat until well-mixed and pour into pan. Bake for 15 minutes or until brown. Bread will be flat.

Hollandaise:

6 egg yolks   salt to taste
juice from half a lemon   Tabasco sauce to taste
3 cups clarified butter

Whisk egg yolks briskly over double boiler of hot (not boiling) water until they are pale yellow and thick. Whisk in lemon juice and remove from heat. Slowly add butter, whisking constantly. Season with salt and Tabasco sauce.

Oysters:

½ cup dry white wine   2 tablespoons butter
3 teaspoons oyster liquor   3 ounces Smithfield ham,
¼ teaspoon lemon juice   sliced paper-thin
1 pint shucked oysters

In a small saucepan, combine white wine with oyster liquor and lemon juice. Heat to a simmer and add oysters. Cook until sides of oysters curl. Remove from heat.

Heat butter in a skillet and slightly sauté ham. Remove ham. Cut corn cakes into serving squares and grill them in the skillet. Place corn cakes on warm plates and add equal portions of ham; spoon oysters on ham and top with a generous dollop of hollandaise. Serves 4.

SAM MILLER'S WAREHOUSE
Richmond

SAM MILLER'S
WAREHOUSE

Since my original visit, Sam Miller's Warehouse has taken on an entirely new personality. Upon entering the newly redecorated restaurant, I was greeted by a warm, mahogany staircase leading to the Captain Morgan Room. The plush carpet and mahogany chairs have added to the comfort and the atmosphere in Shockoe Slip's oldest restaurant. Sam Miller's still has its old rough-hewn walls where meat and poultry once hung on meat hooks. The restaurant is adorned with an interesting array of antiques and bits of history. Black-and-white photographs dating from the Civil War to the turn of the century and old stock certificates and bills of sale dot the walls. Also featured are such nautical artifacts as a ship's wheel and propeller, which are appropriate considering that Sam Miller's prides itself on being the "finest fresh Chesapeake Bay seafood restaurant in Richmond."

The wooden tables that were once bare are now set with crisp white linen tablecloths and handsome silverware. The staff wears semiformal attire. Altogether, the scene at Sam Miller's is decidedly upscale.

You will be pleased to discover that the excellent quality of the cuisine has not changed. Sam Miller's famous Crab Soup is still a favorite with old and new customers alike. Prime Rib is cooked to one's specifications in the traditional style, and the seafood is the freshest available. The Crab Imperial is gloriously rich and fulfilling. The menu changes frequently with the seasons. It's best to wait and see what their menu offers before making up your mind.

Sam Miller's Warehouse is located at 1210 East Cary Street in Richmond's Shockoe Slip. Meals are served from 11:00 a.m. until 11:00 p.m., Monday through Saturday. Sunday brunch is served from 11:00 a.m. until 5:00 p.m. Sandwiches are served every evening until 1:00 a.m. The Captain Morgan Room features live music Wednesday through Sunday nights. For reservations (recommended) call (804) 643-1301.

SAM MILLER'S CRAB IMPERIAL

Imperial Sauce:

2 egg whites　　　　　　　**pinch of white pepper**
pinch of sugar　　　　　　**¾ cup light mayonnaise**

Whip egg whites by hand in a medium-sized bowl until stiff. Add sugar and pepper. Blend in mayonnaise until well-combined.

Crab Mixture:

1 large egg　　　　　　　　**1 teaspoon Old Bay**
dash of Worcestershire　　　　**seasoning**
**　sauce**　　　　　　　　　　**1 pound backfin crabmeat**
½ cup light mayonnaise　　**4 teaspoons melted butter**
pinch of white pepper

Combine egg, Worcestershire sauce, mayonnaise, pepper and Old Bay seasoning in a medium-sized bowl. Carefully stir in crab meat so it does not break down. Divide crabmeat mixture into 4 portions and place in greased, ovenproof ramekins or place entire quantity in a 1½-quart greased casserole dish. Spoon melted butter over mixture and cook in a preheated 375- to 400-degree oven for about 10 minutes. Add 2 tablespoons of Imperial Sauce to each ramekin or ½ cup to the casserole dish if cooking as a whole. Place under broiler just long enough to brown. Serves 4.

SAM MILLER'S CRAB SOUP

4 tablespoons butter or
   margarine
3/4 cup onions, chopped
1 1/2 cups all-purpose flour,
   sifted
1 gallon milk, heated
1 teaspoon chicken base

1/2 teaspoon white pepper
1/2 teaspoon thyme, crushed
1 pint half-and-half cream
3/4 cup cooking sherry
1 pound crabmeat

Melt butter in a 5-quart Dutch oven or other large pot and sauté onions until translucent. Slowly add flour, stirring constantly to maintain smoothness. Stir in milk continuously and very slowly to prevent lumps. Add chicken base, white pepper and thyme. Gradually stir in cream. Continue to stir until soup thickens; stir in sherry and crabmeat until heated through. Yields over 1 gallon.

THE TOBACCO COMPANY
RESTAURANT
Richmond

THE TOBACCO COMPANY RESTAURANT

A first-time excursion to The Tobacco Company is tantamount to a saucy flirtation with Southern history. Passing an ancient wooden Indian on the main floor, you immediately experience the triple-tier effect of an atrium reaching all the way to the skylight roof on the third floor. Visually stunning, this architectural feat bathes each floor with an airy lightness that embellishes the regal austerity of the restaurant's Victorian antiques.

Before dining in this 1878 tobacco warehouse, take the scenic tour. You can either climb the recycled stairway from Richmond's Saint Luke's Hospital or make your ascent in the brass elevator. Arriving on the top floor, a greenhouse solarium decorated with white wicker renders the feeling that you are picnicking in an old Southern garden. The second floor offers little offices for private dining. I was lucky to get a table by the balcony, affording me a panoramic view of the restaurant and its twelve-foot brass chandelier that hangs from the skylight. While I awaited my meal, someone unraveled the Tobacco Company's "sheik story" for me.

One day the restaurant received a call from a man who identified himself as a State Department official. He told them to expect an Arab oil tycoon for dinner. Hours later, the press began to camp out as "security personnel" came to check out the kitchen. Finally, a man attired in an Arab costume, complete with sunglasses, arrived in a Rolls Royce. His "Exxon security," plus a phalanx of news photographers, surrounded his entourage as they were shuttled to a private dining area. That evening the sheik dined in the style of a tycoon, and in tune with Arabic convention, did not speak. As it turned out, he was not a sheik, but a Roanoke school teacher whose friends had aided him in accomplishing this elaborate hoax.

I wondered if the teacher, while dining as a sheik, had ordered the Veal Piccata, which is, to my taste buds, a royal offering. The staff doesn't remember his entree, but they do recall that a number of fine wines were consumed.

162

The next time I'm in Richmond I plan to spend some time in their nightclub below the main level. It features a disc jockey, dancing and hors d'oeuvres. But of course I'll take another tour upstairs because a single visit isn't sufficient to take in all the memorabilia that imparts this restaurant's romance with the past.

The Tobacco Company Restaurant is located at 1201 East Cary Street in Richmond's Shockoe Slip. Lunch is served from 11:30 a.m. until 2:30 p.m., Monday through Saturday. Dinner is served from 5:30 p.m. until 10:30 p.m, Monday through Friday, from 5:00 p.m. until midnight on Saturday and from 5:00 p.m. until 10:30 p.m. on Sunday. Sunday brunch is served from 10:30 a.m. until 2:00 p.m. The Tobacco Company Club is open nightly Tuesday through Sunday. Reservations are accepted for lunch, Sunday brunch and the first hour of dinner service. Call (804) 643-6560.

THE TOBACCO COMPANY RESTAURANT'S
PASTA LIGHT-LINE SALAD

3 quarts water
1 tablespoon salt
1 teaspoon salad oil
8 ounces seashell pasta
1 large zucchini, peeled and
   sliced
½ bunch broccoli
   flowerettes
2 carrots, sliced
1 egg

4 radish roses
2 cups spinach, stemmed
   and steamed
½ cup herb dressing (from
   your grocery)
1 tomato, sliced
4 tablespoons Parmesan
   cheese
20 black pitted olives

Bring water, salt and salad oil to a boil in a large pot. Gradually add pasta and continue to boil, uncovered, until pasta is tender (about 15 minutes). Drain, rinse with cold water, and chill. Steam zucchini, broccoli and carrots approximately 2 to 3 minutes. Boil an egg. Make radish roses. Toss pasta with cleaned and chilled spinach, steamed and cooled vegetables and herb dressing. Garnish with tomatoes, radishes, egg slices, Parmesan cheese and black olives. Serves 4 to 6.

THE TOBACCO COMPANY RESTAURANT'S VEAL PICCATA

flour for veal
4 2- to 3-ounce veal cutlets, thinly sliced and pounded flat
1 egg, beaten
½ cup bread crumbs
½ cup Romano cheese

2 tablespoons butter
juice of 1 lemon
½ cup mushrooms, sliced
4 tablespoons red wine
1 cup Demi-Glace (recipe follows)

Lightly flour veal and dip in an egg wash; dip veal in bread crumbs and Romano cheese. Sauté in butter until each side has browned. Splash veal with lemon juice and remove from pan. Add the mushrooms to pan and sauté briefly. Add wine and Demi-Glace. Simmer to reduce slightly. Pour sauce over veal. Serves 4.

Demi-Glace:
1 cup brown sauce
1 cup beef stock

½ cup Marsala wine

Combine brown sauce, beef stock and Marsala wine. Mix well.

TRAVELLER'S RESTAURANT
Richmond

TRAVELLER'S RESTAURANT

As I opened the original iron gate of General Lee's first post–Civil War home, it didn't immediately occur to me that Traveller was so well-known. Later, in the converted main dining room that was once Traveller's stable, I tried in vain to recall the names of other general's horses. Lee considered Traveller special, describing his feelings in this way: "If I were an artist, . . . I would draw a true picture of Traveller. . . . Such a picture would inspire a poet. . . . But I am no artist; I can only say he is a Confederate gray."

As I entered through the bar, which is part of the basement of the main house, I saw a handsome, black marble fireplace with Lee's portrait hanging above it, appropriately enough. Another portrait of Lee at age thirty-three can be seen nearby in a small dining room, but the dining room that intrigued me most was the one called the General's Office. Many think Lee received guests who tried to persuade him to begin another war. Although there is no proof, the layout of the house suggests that he may have received them in this room.

Settling down in the two-tiered main dining room, accentuated with wood paneling, bright green tablecloths and equestrian prints and oils, I ordered their Lamb with Raspberry Sauce. Lamb has such a distinctive taste that I wasn't sure how raspberry sauce would go with it, but I was surprised to find myself preferring it to the usual mint. Though I sampled small amounts, large portions of food are the norm here. Seafood enthusiasts will enjoy their fresh Crab Imperial, served only when backfin crab is available.

Desserts are my downfall, and theirs proved to be exceptional. I tried to take only one bite each of their tasty Chocolate Mousse Pie, New York Cheesecake and Pecan Pie, but lost my battle with the Pecan, which they give a true Southern rendering.

Adjacent to this dining room is another in a lovely brick courtyard where Matthew Brady took the famous photograph of Lee at the back door. Lee lived only four months in this home, which was lent to him by the Stuarts after his own was confiscated. He moved to Dinwiddie County to be less accessible to those who did not share his belief that " . . . All should unite in honest efforts to obliterate the effects of war and restore the blessings of peace."

Traveller's Restaurant is located at 707 East Franklin Street in Richmond. Lunch is served from 11:30 a.m. until 2:30 p.m., Monday through Friday. Dinner is served from 5:30 p.m. until 10:00 p.m., Monday through Saturday. For reservations (suggested) call (804) 644-1040.

TRAVELLER'S LAMB WITH RASPBERRY SAUCE

1 pint raspberries or 1 10-ounce package frozen raspberries, thawed
½ cup currant jelly
2 tablespoons cold water

1 tablespoon cornstarch
⅓ cup Chambord liqueur
2 or more tablespoons butter
2 pounds thick lamb chops

Blend raspberries, jelly, water and cornstarch in a blender or a food processor with a steel blade until pureed. Pour into saucepan and cook over low heat, stirring until clear. Add liqueur and stir until slightly thickened. Heat butter in a skillet and pan-fry lamb on both sides. Do not overcook; lamb should be slightly rare. Place a ladle of sauce in each plate and place lamb over sauce. Serves 4.

TRAVELLER'S CRAB IMPERIAL

1 pound backfin crabmeat	1 teaspoon Old Bay
1 egg	Seafood seasoning
⅓ cup mayonnaise	white pepper to taste
1 teaspoon dry mustard	dash of cayenne pepper
1 teaspoon lemon juice	

Pick over crab meat carefully to remove any remaining shell or cartilage. In a small bowl, combine all ingredients except crab meat, stirring into a sauce. Reserve 4 teaspoons of sauce. Toss crab meat and sauce lightly. Spoon crab meat into individual, greased mini-casseroles. Top each with 1 teaspoon of sauce. Bake in a preheated 350-degree oven for 15 to 20 minutes. Serves 4.

HALF WAY HOUSE
Petersburg

HALF WAY HOUSE Yes, George Washington did sleep here. So did Robert E. Lee and Ulysses S. Grant (thankfully, not at the same time). Built in 1760 on a land grant from George II of England, the Half Way House, located halfway between Petersburg and Richmond, served as a stagecoach stop and ordinary. An ordinary was a lodge that assigned sleeping space according to a traveler's station in life. The guests slept upstairs dormitory-style and ate downstairs in the Gentlemen's Tap Room. The kitchen was then, as it is today, in a separate building just a stone's throw from the dining room. In those days, the cooks were not only expected to transport the food but also to whistle or sing in the process. This supposedly prevented food from being snitched along the way. Today, the food is still speedily transferred to your table, but the whistling has long since gone by the boards.

To enter the dining room, you must walk down the original brick steps, worn smooth from centuries of famous footsteps. Whether your footsteps add another famed note to this dining room is of little consequence to the headwaiter, James, who has been here for forty-two years. James greets everyone with the graciousness that defines true Southern hospitality.

A cool mist fell the evening I visited, giving the fireplaces an extra dimension of welcome in this room that clearly reveres the simplicity of the past.

Seated beside a calico-curtained window, I had a glass of Colonial Hot Spiced Wine, accompanied by exquisite little Cinnamon Rolls—a tasty way to warm your bones. This was followed by an excellent appetizer of homemade Vegetable Soup. Their Filet Mignon, served with Virginia peanuts and fried shrimp, is delicious. I also sampled the Green Beans— so good I asked for their recipe. I also recommend their colonial Gingerbread with Hard Sauce for dessert.

The wine selection, like the atmosphere, is simple but excellent. As I sat enjoying a glass of after-dinner wine, I felt that I had moved back to a time when moments were savored like slow sips of wine.

The Half Way House is located at 10301 Jefferson Davis Highway between Petersburg and Richmond. Lunch is served from 11:30 a.m. until 2:00 p.m., Sunday through Friday. Dinner is served from 5:30 p.m. until 9:30 p.m. Sunday through Thursday, and from 5:30 p.m. until 10:00 p.m. on Friday and Saturday. For reservations (recommended) call (804) 275-1760.

HALF WAY HOUSE'S HOT SPICED WINE

1 quart dry red wine
1 cup water
1 cup sugar
1 teaspoon whole cloves
1 cinnamon stick
1 lemon, sliced
½ of orange, sliced

Combine all ingredients in a large pot. Bring to boil over high heat, then simmer for 15 minutes. Strain and serve hot. Serves 10.

HALF WAY HOUSE'S GREEN BEANS

6 strips bacon
1 medium onion, finely
 chopped
4 tomatoes, chopped
2 tablespoons sugar
salt and pepper to taste
2 16-ounce cans of French-
 style green beans

Fry bacon until crisp. Fry onions in bacon grease until light brown. Add tomatoes, sugar, salt and pepper. Simmer until tomatoes are soft. Add beans and continue to simmer until heated through. Crumble bacon and add just before serving. Serves 8 to 10.

HALF WAY HOUSE'S FRENCH DRESSING

1 cup cider vinegar
2 teaspoons paprika
½ tablespoon dry, ground
   mustard

2 teaspoons sugar
1 garlic clove, minced
1 cup cotton seed oil
¼ onion, quartered

Mix vinegar, paprika, mustard, sugar and garlic until thoroughly incorporated. Add oil and blend in blender. Add onion to dressing and allow to set overnight in refrigerator. Remove onion and serve. Yields 2 cups.

CHOWNING'S TAVERN
Williamsburg

CHOWNING'S TAVERN

Spreading the loosely woven napkin in my lap reminded me of how long it took our colonial ancestors to weave just one small square of fabric. And, for that matter, how long it took them to prepare one meal. Yet, even without our modern shortcuts, they did reserve time for enjoying themselves, even the common folk.

Chowning's catered to the tastes of the working man with grogs and ales served then, as they are today, in blue and white salt-glazed mugs. The food was most likely fresh fish and game heaped on pewter plates.

The current waiters are dressed in red knee breeches, but I'll bet in 1766 when Josiah Chowning opened the doors of his tavern, the servants were more simply attired. Today's reconstructed building and interior furnishings of sturdy wood tables and chairs are not, however, unlike those that Chowning would have provided for his patrons. Even the cartoons on the walls attest to the merrymaking that goes on after nine o'clock when Chowning's becomes Gambols. The atmosphere reverts to an eighteenth-century tavern complete with magician. Guests are encouraged to enter into games of Goose and Loo that are played quite literally for peanuts.

I missed the evening entertainment, but thoroughly enjoyed having lunch upstairs beneath a dormer window. I had been told that their Welsh Rarebit is exceptional, and it is, but my favorite dish of all is the Black Walnut Ice Cream. I remembered that particular ice cream from several summers ago when I lunched outdoors under Chowning's grape arbor canopy. On that very hot day I strongly appreciated a Mint Julep from the bar and a light Chicken Salad Plate.

For the evening fare, the favored dish is Roast Prime Rib of Beef. Chowning's Good Bread and their garden salad with a special Chutney Dressing are popular, also. My suggestion to you would be to go late enough to stay and join in an eighteenth-century evening of fun and spirits when Chowning's changes into Gambols.

174

Chowning's Tavern is located on the Duke of Gloucester Street in Williamsburg. Lunch is served daily from 10:30 a.m. until 2:30 p.m., and dinner is served from 5:00 p.m. until 9:30 p.m. Gambols is open from 9:00 p.m. until 1:00 a.m. Winter hours may vary. For reservations (required for Chowning's but not accepted for Gambols) call (804) 229-2141.

CHOWNING'S TAVERN'S BLACK WALNUT ICE CREAM

8 egg yolks
1¼ cups sugar
dash of salt
2 cups milk
2 cups whipping cream

1 teaspoon black walnut
  extract
1 cup black walnuts,
  chopped

Beat the egg yolks with the sugar until creamy; add the salt. In a saucepan bring the milk and cream almost to boiling, but do not boil. Remove from heat and pour slowly into the egg mixture, stirring constantly. Add the black walnut extract. Heat to scalding. Pour the mixture into a one-gallon freezer container of an ice cream maker. Follow the manufacturer's instructions for freezing. When the dasher is removed, add the black walnuts, stirring to distribute them evenly. Pack as freezing instructions direct and allow to "ripen" at least 3 hours before serving. Yields 1½ quarts.

CHOWNING'S TAVERN'S WELSH RAREBIT

1 tablespoon butter
1 pound sharp Cheddar
  cheese, grated
¾ cup beer
dash of cayenne pepper (or
  Tabasco sauce)

1 teaspoon dry mustard
½ teaspoon salt
½ teaspoon Worcestershire
  sauce
1 egg, slightly beaten
1 teaspoon cornstarch

Melt butter in the top of a double boiler. Add the cheese and all but one tablespoon of beer. Cook over hot (but not boiling) water until the cheese melts. Combine the seasonings with the remaining tablespoon of beer and the Worcestershire sauce, and stir into the cheese. Combine the slightly beaten egg with the cornstarch; stir into the cheese mixture and let it thicken slightly. Serve immediately over toast or broiled tomato halves. Serves 4.

CHOWNING'S TAVERN'S WINE COOLER

¾ cup lemonade   sprig of mint
¼ cup dry red wine   maraschino cherry

Pour the lemonade over crushed ice in 10-ounce tumbler, then add the red wine. Garnish with a sprig of mint and a cherry. Serves 1.

CHRISTIANA CAMPBELL'S TAVERN
Williamsburg

CHRISTIANA CAMPBELL'S TAVERN

Of all the taverns in Williamsburg, Christiana Campbell's 1771 hostelry, according to George Washington's diary, was his favorite. Whether he was lured by the food, the accommodations at this "good dwelling house" or the plump and bawdy Mrs. Campbell, known for her earthy tales and humor, history does not say; it only hints. I must say, though, that reading between the lines certainly casts a less austere profile on the age. They really had a good time, as I did the morning I brunched here.

The gambrel-roofed, colonial frame house has been faithfully reconstructed. Early records indicate a blue-gray décor, imitated today right down to the checked linen curtains and the original Lambeth delftware, reproduced for this restaurant only.

I'm always fascinated by obscure differences, and the sugar container on the wooden table caught my eye. A reproduction from the tavern's early days, it is called a "muffin ear" and pours from the center.

I began brunch with the very best Pecan Waffles I've ever tasted, along with a side order of tiny, Sweet Potato Muffins that won't let you stop with just one. Then, because I'd never tasted Fig Ice Cream, I sampled this very unusual dessert. Equally delicious was their Rum Cream Pie.

What a calorie binge! I could have had a much lighter meal with their version of the colonial Salmagundi (chef's salad) for lunch or their unique Shad Roe Omelet.

If you go for dinner you'll be entertained by strolling minstrels. Because the tavern focuses on seafood from the Chesapeake Bay, my dinner suggestion would be their popular A Made Dish of Shrimp and Lobster or the Deviled Backfin Crabmeat.

Although I rarely choose a mixed drink, their Black Velvet Cocktail, an elixir of champagne and Guinness Stout, does pose an intriguing invitation. But then, I found the entire personality of the tavern to be a warm invitation to another age.

Christiana Campbell's Tavern is located on Waller Street in Williamsburg. Brunch is served daily from 11:00 a.m. until 2:30 p.m., and dinner from 5:30 p.m. until 9:30 p.m. Winter hours may vary. For reservations (required for dinner) call (800) HISTORY.

CHRISTIANA CAMPBELL'S TAVERN'S
SWEET POTATO MUFFINS

⅔ cup canned or fresh
  cooked sweet potatoes,
  well drained
4 tablespoons butter
½ cup sugar
1 egg
¾ cup all-purpose flour
2 teaspoons baking powder

½ teaspoon salt
½ teaspoon cinnamon
¼ teaspoon nutmeg
½ cup milk
4 tablespoons pecans or
  walnuts, chopped
4 tablespoons raisins,
  chopped

Preheat oven to 400 degrees. Grease muffin tins that are 1½ inches in diameter. Purée the sweet potatoes in a food processor or blender. Cream the butter and sugar. Beat in the egg and puréed sweet potatoes. Sift the flour with the baking powder, salt, cinnamon and nutmeg. Add dry ingredients alternately by hand with the milk, chopped nuts and raisins, mixing just until blended. Do not overmix. Spoon into the greased muffin tins, filling each completely full. A little sugar and cinnamon may be sprinkled on top of each muffin, if desired. Bake at 400 degrees for 25 minutes. Yields 30 muffins.

CHRISTIANA CAMPBELL'S TAVERN'S
RUM CREAM PIE

1 envelope unflavored
  gelatin
½ cup cold water
5 egg yolks
1 cup sugar
⅓ cup dark rum

1½ cups whipping cream
1 9-inch graham cracker pie
  crust
unsweetened chocolate for
  garnish

Soften the gelatin in ½ cup of cold water. Place over low heat and bring almost to a boil, stirring to dissolve. Beat the egg yolks and sugar until very light. Stir the gelatin into the egg mixture; cool. Gradually add the rum, beating constantly. In separate bowl whip the cream until it stands in soft peaks and fold it into the gelatin mixture. Cool until the mixture begins to set, then spoon it into the crumb crust and chill until firm enough to cut. Grate the unsweetened chocolate over the top before serving. Yields 1 pie.

CHRISTIANA CAMPBELL'S TAVERN'S
A MADE DISH OF SHRIMP AND LOBSTER

1½ green peppers, quartered
3 medium tomatoes
1 6-ounce package long-grain rice
1 6-ounce package wild rice
½ pound fresh mushrooms, quartered
¼ pound butter, divided
¾ pound lobster, cooked and shelled
1 pound shrimp, cooked and cleaned
1 15½-ounce can pearl onions
¾ cup dry sherry
1 teaspoon lemon juice
Worcestershire sauce to taste
salt and white pepper to taste
parsley, chopped (optional)

Partially cook the green pepper in boiling water, remove from water and cut the quarters in half. Reserve. Scald tomatoes in boiling water for 60 seconds; drain, remove skin and cut in half. Squeeze out and discard tomato juice and seeds and cut each half into 4 pieces. Reserve. Mix the two kinds of rice and cook according to package instructions. Set aside. Sauté the mushrooms quickly in a small amount of butter and reserve. Cut the lobster into bite-sized pieces. Melt the remaining butter over medium heat and sauté the lobster, shrimp and onions. Add the sherry, lemon juice and seasonings. Add the green pepper, tomatoes and mushrooms and simmer over low heat, stirring gently, until heated through. Arrange the seafood and vegetables in a heated serving dish with rice. Garnish with chopped parsley if desired. Serves 4 to 6.

KING'S ARMS TAVERN
Williamsburg

KING'S ARMS TAVERN

Guests are probably more apt to notice the classical decorating that enhances the bright Williamsburg green fireplaces and moldings at the King's Arms rather than the obscure architectural feature of reversed balusters on the stairs. I was fascinated to find that the seventh and thirteenth balusters were purposely turned upside down. There are two theories. The first is that they were positioned in opposition to the others to ward off evil spirits; the second holds that colonial people purposely built in flaws to reaffirm their belief that only God was perfect.

Hence, when the tavern was replicated on its 1770 site, historically sensitive architects complied with the early colonial beliefs.

Historical research reveals that Jane Vobe operated the King's Arms, reputedly one of the most genteel taverns in the city. The Virginia aristocracy was fed with Travis House Oyster Pie, Colonial Game Pie, Cream of Peanut Soup and Sally Lunn Bread. These colonial dishes continue to serve such important guests as Queen Elizabeth, Theodore Hess and a former Secretary of State. A waiter, who served the Secretary, asked if he would like to have the bill sent to his home, to which the Secretary enthusiastically replied, "Yes, I would." The waiter then asked, "Your home address, sir?" The Secretary looked puzzled, turned to his wife and asked, "Where do we live?" Is it any wonder our foreign policy has problems?

The day I lunched at the tavern, I had no problem in choosing the refreshing Frosted Fruit Shrub and Chicken Pot Pie, one of their celebrated colonial dishes. To my pleasure, the pie had no resemblance to the frozen variety found in supermarkets. Had I wanted a lighter meal, I could have had their King's Arms Salad Bowl with strips of Smithfield ham, turkey, cheese and their house dressing. Instead, I went right to a dessert of Colonial Meringue with fresh strawberries—exactly the right light touch.

The tavern would be an excellent evening choice with its

good selection of fine wines and beers and strolling balladeers who perform with lutes and sing merry songs of colonial days.

King's Arms Tavern is located on the Duke of Gloucester Street in Williamsburg. Lunch is served from 11:30 a.m. until 2:30 p.m. Dinner is served from 5:15 p.m. until 8:00 p.m. on weeknights and from 5:15 p.m. until 9:30 p.m. on weekends and holidays. Lunch and dinner are served daily from April through December; check on winter serving hours. For dinner reservations (required) call (804) 229-2141.

KING'S ARMS TAVERN'S CHICKEN POT PIE

2 chickens (2½ to 3 pounds each)
2 ribs of celery, chopped
1 medium onion, sliced
1 bay leaf
1 teaspoon salt
½ teaspoon white pepper
½ cup butter
½ cup all-purpose flour
1 10-ounce package frozen peas, cooked

4 ribs celery, diced and cooked
4 carrots, sliced and cooked
1¾ cups potatoes, diced and cooked
1 egg
2 tablespoons milk
Pastry Crust (recipe below)

Preheat the oven to 375 degrees 10 minutes before the pies are to go in. Grease 8 individual casseroles. Put the chicken on to cook in a large pan with enough water to cover. Add 2 chopped ribs of celery, onion, bay leaf, salt and pepper. Bring the water to a boil, reduce the heat to simmer, and cook until the chicken is done. Remove the fat and strain the stock. Cut chicken into large pieces. In a saucepan melt the butter and stir in flour. Cook 5 minutes, stirring constantly. Add enough chicken stock, stirring constantly, to achieve a light and creamy consistency. Simmer 5 minutes. Add salt and pepper to taste. Divide the chicken and cooked vegetables equally into 8 individual casseroles. Add to each the amount of sauce desired, stirring the chicken and vegetables to mix thoroughly. Mix egg and milk together. Cover each casserole with pastry,

183

brush with the egg mixture and puncture pastry with a fork to allow steam to escape. Bake at 375 degrees until crust is golden brown. Serves 8.

Pastry Crust:

3 cups all-purpose flour   1 cup shortening
1 teaspoon salt   ice water
2 teaspoons sugar

Mix the dry ingredients together. Blend in the shortening with knives or a pastry blender until the mixture is of pebbly consistency. Store in a covered container in refrigerator. When ready to use, moisten the pastry mix with enough ice water to hold the dough together and divide into 8 equal portions. Roll out on a lightly floured board.

KING'S ARMS TAVERN'S TENDERLOIN OF BEEF STUFFED WITH OYSTERS

4 7-ounce tenderloin steaks   4 slices bacon
12 medium oysters   1 teaspoon parsley, chopped
salt and pepper to taste   (or fresh chives, snipped)
3 tablespoons butter,
   divided

Insert a sharp knife into the side of each tenderloin steak and, with a short sawing motion, make a pocket. Season the oysters with salt and pepper; sauté in 1 tablespoon butter and some of the oyster liquid only until the edges begin to curl; drain. Stuff each steak with three oysters, wrap with a slice of bacon and secure with a toothpick. Broil or sauté. Heat the remaining butter until light brown, add the parsley or chives, and pour over the cooked steaks. Serves 4.

THE WILLIAMSBURG INN
Williamsburg

WILLIAMSBURG INN

This genteel inn, modeled from the English Regency period, was built initially for scholars who came to study the restoration of Williamsburg. In past years, the inn has become better known as a sort of "decompression chamber." Only a helicopter ride away from Washington, it is now the official resting place for visiting foreign dignitaries suffering from jet lag.

As you enter this insular oasis via the circular drive, you are greeted by a doorman whose warm service adds to the regal feeling you get in the presence of tasteful grandeur. Maybe it's the Regency décor's oriental influence that renders a subtle tranquility. You inwardly murmur, "Oh yes, I could get used to this." Then, you come upon a family portrait, complete with servants, from the eighteenth century. Today, the painting you see has been restored to the original, but when it was found some years ago, the original black faces of the servants had been painted over with white. Apparently, the inheritors of the painting tried to repaint history to reflect the needs of their time. The restorers have unmasked the cover-up, and today the painting hangs above the stairway near the entrance to the Regency Dining Room.

As I walked into the dining room I could understand why the VIP's of the world dine here. A sea of silver, gleaming beneath candlelight, sets the mood for a relaxing evening. Cocktails, with an appetizer of Smoked Salmon, tweaked my taste buds for the succulent Rack of Lamb, which I enjoyed with a light dry wine. My dinner companion chose a lower-calorie Poached Salmon that offered a lovely presentation. Then, while enjoying this classic American cuisine with continental overtones, the room was engulfed with music. An orchestra dramatically ascended into the room from the floor below. Had I not been so surprised, I would have applauded. Before dessert, which I will verbally applaud, my dinner companion introduced me to Stilton cheese—a delicious discovery.

I sampled four desserts, which included the Pecan Bar,

Black Forest Cake, Rum Cream Pie and a Sacher-Torte. To choose the best is like deciding which of your children you love the most.

I could easily spend a week at this five-star hotel, and most of that time would be spent in the Regency Room.

The Williamsburg Inn is located on Francis Street. Meals are served daily. Breakfast is served from 7:30 a.m. until 10:00 a.m. Lunch is served from noon until 2:00 p.m. in the Regency Room and from 11:30 a.m. until 3:00 p.m. in the Lounge. Dinner is served from 6:30 p.m. until 9:30 p.m. in the summer and from 6:00 p.m. until 9:00 p.m. in the winter. Sunday brunch is served from noon until 1:30 p.m. For reservations (required for dinner) call (804) 229-1000.

THE WILLIAMSBURG INN'S PECAN BARS

¾ cup butter	3 cups sifted all-purpose
¾ cup sugar	flour
2 eggs	½ teaspoon baking powder
rind of one lemon, grated	

Cream the butter and sugar; add the eggs and lemon rind and beat well. Sift the flour and baking powder together; add to the creamed mixture and beat well. Chill the dough until it is firm enough to handle. Preheat the oven to 375 degrees. Press the dough onto the bottom of two greased and floured 9-inch by 9-inch by 2-inch pans and prick all over with a fork. Bake 12 to 15 minutes or until the dough looks half done. Remove from the oven and set aside.

Pecan Topping:

1 cup butter	1 cup honey
1 cup light brown sugar, packed	¼ cup whipping cream
	3 cups pecans, chopped

Reduce oven to 350 degrees. Put the butter, sugar and honey in a deep, heavy saucepan; boil, stirring for 5 minutes. Remove from heat. Cool slightly and add the cream and

187

chopped pecans; mix well. Spread the topping evenly over the surface of the partially baked dough with a greased wooden spoon. Bake for 30 to 35 minutes. Cool and cut into 1-inch by 2-inch bars. Yields 54 bars.

THE WILLIAMSBURG INN'S FANTASIO OMELET

1 medium apple	3 eggs
1 slice stale bread	1 tablespoon light cream
¼ cup butter, divided	salt and pepper to taste
2 ounces sausage	¼ cup Cheddar cheese,
1 teaspoon chopped walnuts	shredded
or pecans	

Peel and dice the apple. Trim the bread and cut into croutons. Fry the croutons until brown and crisp in 1 tablespoon of butter, turning to brown all sides; reserve. Crumble the sausage and sauté until cooked through; drain and reserve. Sauté the apple in the sausage drippings and, when it is almost done, add the chopped nuts. Combine the croutons, sausage, apple and nuts; set aside. Beat the eggs and cream together until the mixture is light and foamy. Add salt and pepper to taste. Heat the remaining butter in an omelet pan over high heat; remove the pan from heat. Add the eggs and return to heat. When the eggs begin to set, lift the edges with a fork or spatula so that any uncooked egg will run to the bottom of the pan. Shake the pan occasionally to prevent sticking. When eggs are set, mound the apple mixture and the cheese on half of the omelet; fold it, and roll it onto a plate. Serves 2 to 3.

SMITHFIELD INN AND TAVERN
Smithfield

SMITHFIELD INN
AND TAVERN

Built in 1752, the Smithfield Inn and Tavern has operated as an "ordinary," tavern or public house for the majority of its existence. Today, under owners Jerry Turner and Deborah Shilling, the Smithfield Inn boasts three dining rooms—two in the original structure and one in the addition built in 1922.

On the October evening that I dined at the inn, there was a crispness in the air. Maybe it was because I had not yet acclimated to cool weather, but the crackling fire in the parlor fireplace seemed especially inviting. As I warmed by the fire in a parlor tastefully decorated with eighteenth-century period furnishings, I was greeted by the faint aroma of baking ham.

The ham, or to be precise, Smithfield Ham, has been one of the inn's major draws for many years. As a matter of fact, during John D. Rockefeller's restoration of Williamsburg, Rockefeller himself was tempted by the ham's reputation. The story goes that Rockefeller arrived shortly after the proprietor, Mrs. Sykes, had installed air conditioning. Noticing that Rockefeller had left the dining-room door open, the forthright Mrs. Sykes allegedly asked, "Mr. Rockefeller, do you know how much it costs to air-condition a room?" Rockefeller nodded. "Well, then, if you do, close the door," Mrs. Sykes said, and that obedient gentleman did as he was told.

Naturally, I ordered the Smithfield Ham, which was accompanied by Smithfield-style Stewed Tomatoes, Black-eyed Peas, Green Beans, Biscuits and Fried Corn Bread. The ham has a distinctive taste that cannot be compared to any ham I've ever eaten, thanks to the method by which it is cured and cooked. I actually preferred the ham layered between biscuits or corn bread. A dry red wine might help to acquaint you with the ham. The tomatoes were especially sweet, as was their popular Coconut Raisin Pie, which was so rich you could gain weight just by looking at it.

After an evening at the inn, I felt as if I had been up North for a long time and had come home to appreciate the warmth and manners of the South again.

Smithfield Inn and Tavern is located at 112 Main Street in Smithfield. Dinner is served from 5:00 p.m. until 9:00 p.m. Wednesday through Saturday and from noon until 5:00 p.m. on Sunday. The tavern is open from 11:00 a.m. until 11:00 p.m. For reservations call (804) 357-0244.

SMITHFIELD INN AND TAVERN'S
STEWED TOMATOES

1 pound canned tomatoes	2 tablespoons flour
1/3 cup brown and white sugar, mixed	1 teaspoon vanilla
	1/2 cup butter
1 teaspoon cinnamon	2 biscuits

Place undrained tomatoes in a bowl with sugar, cinnamon, flour and vanilla. Mix until well-blended. Pour into a greased, deep casserole. Chop butter into tablespoon-sized pieces and dot on top. Crumble biscuits and sprinkle over top or add to mixture. Bake in a preheated 375-degree oven for 45 to 55 minutes. Serves 4 to 6.

SMITHFIELD INN AND TAVERN'S
COCONUT RAISIN PIE

1 cup coconut	1 teaspoon vinegar
1/2 cup raisins	1 teaspoon vanilla
1 1/2 cups sugar	9-inch pie shell
2 eggs	whipped cream or vanilla
1/2 cup butter	ice cream

Mix coconut, raisins, sugar, eggs, butter, vinegar and vanilla with an electric mixer or a blender until well-blended. Pour into unbaked pie shell. Bake in a preheated 350-degree oven for 30 minutes. Remove from oven and cool for 15 to 20 minutes before cutting. Serve with a scoop of whipped cream or vanilla ice cream if desired. Yields 1 pie.

SMITHFIELD INN AND TAVERN'S
SMITHFIELD HAM

1 country ham   **1 cup brown sugar**
1 cup sugar   **1 cup water**

Scrub ham thoroughly. Soak in fresh water for 24 hours. Replace water and soak an additional 12 hours. Place in a large pot and simmer at least 4 hours. Mix sugar, brown sugar and water into a paste-like mixture and coat ham. Place ham in roasting pan with several cups of water. Cover and bake at 350 degrees for 1 hour, turning every 15 minutes. Remove and cool for 1½ hours before cutting.

MILTON WARREN'S
ICE HOUSE RESTAURANT
Virginia Beach

MILTON WARREN'S ICE HOUSE

The psychiatric field would argue about the influence a parent's career has on his or her offspring. But Milton Warren believes that growing up in a dietitian's home provided the impetus that launched him into the restaurant business. Warren's mother instilled the philosophy that makes his restaurant "a place to dine rather than just eat."

Built at the turn of the century, the ice house was insulated with ten- to twelve-inch cork walls and two feet of sawdust in the ceiling. The ingenuity of those early builders never ceases to amaze me. So many materials that current builders throw away were once put to very efficient uses.

Originally, the ice house was built to aid the local fishing industry, then expanded its operation to supply seasonal vacationers and local resort hotels.

The building was fast falling into disrepair when Warren salvaged this page of coastal history and converted the structure into a restaurant.

Sitting in the cozy dining room, Daintry and I were glad that he cared to create this intimate setting. The dining room is decorated with large ice hooks hung on weathered walls, and the tables are attractively set with linen cloths and fresh flowers.

We began by sampling two of their more popular appetizers, the Clam Oreganata and Oysters Rockefeller, and found both satisfied our seafood cravings.

I never think of ordering anything but seafood at the beach, and their Shrimp Scampi proved to be a light and luscious dieter's dream. Even with a nibble of their delicious homemade Popovers, there was still room for a sliver of their rich and creamy Cheesecake.

The restaurant also offers a small but adequate wine and beer selection with a strong emphasis on domestic vintages.

Milton Warren's Ice House is located at 604 Norfolk Avenue in Virginia Beach. Dinner is served daily from 6:00 p.m. until 10:00 p.m. The restaurant is closed on Monday during the winter. For reservations (recommended) call (804) 422-2323.

ICE HOUSE'S CHEESECAKE

Topping:
1 pint sour cream   **2 teaspoons vanilla**
½ cup sugar

Place all ingredients in blender and mix until smooth. Refrigerate.

Pie Crust:
14-ounce package vanilla   **¼ cup butter**
  wafers   **1 teaspoon vanilla**
4 teaspoons sugar

Crush vanilla wafers in blender. Melt butter. In mixing bowl add wafers, sugar, melted butter and vanilla. Combine until well mixed. Press mixture into springform pan, covering bottom and sides. Set aside.

Filling:
3 8-ounce packages cream   **2 cups sugar**
  cheese   **2 teaspoons vanilla**
5 eggs

Soften cream cheese and place in electric blender with eggs, mixing until smooth. Add sugar, gradually, until well incorporated. Add vanilla, mixing to blend through. Pour into prepared crust and cook in a 325-degree oven for one and a half hours. Cool slightly, add topping and cook for another 15 minutes. Cool and place in refrigerator for 24 hours before serving. Yields 1 cake.

ICE HOUSE'S SEAFOOD NEPTUNE

4 tablespoons butter   **4 ounces crabmeat**
¼ cup white wine   **2 1-pound flounder fillets**
4 scallops   **2 tablespoons lemon juice**
4 shrimp, medium (cleaned)   **salt and pepper to taste**

In skillet, add butter and wine simultaneously. Sauté scallops, shrimp and crabmeat about 2 minutes. Slit each flounder along the side to form a pocket. Spoon sautéed mixture into cavities. Place on baking sheet or roasting pan. Pour remaining wine and butter sauce over top of fillets. Add lemon juice and salt and pepper to taste. Bake in 375-degree oven 10 to 15 minutes. Serves 4.

ICE HOUSE'S SHRIMP SCAMPI

4 teaspoons butter
2 ounces oil (olive or
    peanut)
2 to 3 garlic cloves, sliced
1 pound medium shrimp,
    shelled
½ teaspoon lemon juice

½ medium onion, chopped
1 tomato, chopped
½ of green pepper, chopped
1 teaspoon black pepper
1 teaspoon salt
1 tablespoon fresh parsley
¼ cup white wine

In skillet, melt butter, add oil and sauté garlic lightly. Add shrimp, cooking until it turns pink and begins to curl. Add lemon juice, onion, tomato, green pepper, black pepper, salt, parsley and wine. Cook only a minute or so until tender. Remove shrimp and pour sauce from skillet over top. Serves 4.

HILDA CROCKETT'S
CHESAPEAKE HOUSE
Tangier Island

**HILDA CROCKETT'S
CHESAPEAKE HOUSE** After the Captain Thomas ferry docked on Tangier Island, I pretended to wait for my daughter to come ashore. In actuality, I was eavesdropping on the island fishermen tying their nets. I wanted to hear their dialect, said to be an admixture of a Scotch brogue with Old English. The ferryboat captain told me that the self-conscious islanders won't speak to foreigners in that dialect—for outsiders, a totally different Southern dialect is spoken. I listened, and true to the captain's warning, I could not decipher one word.

The dialect, like the island, has an old world quality about it. Little appears to have changed from the early 1600s when Captain John Smith, on an exploratory mission for England, purchased Tangier for the price of two overcoats (a marginally better deal than the Indians got for Manhattan).

Since Tangier's roads are too narrow to permit cars, we walked a few blocks to the Chesapeake House for lunch. The restaurant is better known as Hilda Crockett's. The late Mrs. Crockett was a descendant of one of the early English families who settled the island.

Mrs. Crockett, with only a dime to her name, borrowed the money for the purchase of the white frame house. To make the payments, Mrs. Crockett concentrated on island ingenuity and began offering her delicious fare to hunters and "drummers," as salesmen were then called. Word of mouth spread Mrs. Crockett's fame and, as a consequence, today you have to wait in line for a meal, still made from her recipes.

The family-style meals are served on blue vinyl tablecloths, as fancy accessories would be as out of place in this low key atmosphere as gourmet cooking. We were served Crab Cakes, Clam Fritters, Ham, Potato Salad, Cole Slaw, Applesauce, Corn Custard, Homemade Bread and Pound Cake. There are no alcoholic beverages on the menu. My vote goes to the seafood and Corn Custard, while Daintry feels the Pound Cake deserves more than honorable mention.

After lunch, meandering over to the museum, I discovered that Tangier's first settler, William Crockett, had only a prayer book to read until 1775 when a merchant ship captain gave him a Bible. The islanders were so excited by this gift that nightly readings drew whole families.

Those Bible readings may have produced a long-reaching effect. Over two hundred years have passed, and there is still no alcoholism or need for a jail in this peaceful community. A little pamphlet explains, ". . . our quaint ways may be misunderstood as slow, but time is abundant here and we wish it not away."

Hilda Crockett's Chesapeake House is located on Main Street in Tangier Island. Access to Tangier is provided via the Reedville, Virginia, ferry (804/333-4656) or the Crisfield, Maryland, ferry (301/968-2338). Meals are served daily April 15 through October 15, with breakfast from 7:00 a.m. until 9:00 a.m. and lunch from 11:30 a.m. until 5:00 p.m. For reservations (preferred for tour groups) call (804) 891-2331.

HILDA CROCKETT'S CRAB CAKES

2 slices bread
1 pound crabmeat
1 teaspoon Old Bay
  Seasoning
¼ teaspoon salt
1 tablespoon mayonnaise

1 tablespoon Worcestershire
  sauce
1 egg, beaten
1 teaspoon dry mustard
oil for frying

Break bread into crumbs and moisten with water. In a mixing bowl, combine all ingredients thoroughly. Shape into individual patty cakes and fry in oil until golden brown. Yields 10 to 12 cakes.

HILDA CROCKETT'S CLAM FRITTERS

2 cups clams
1 teaspoon pepper
1 cup pancake flour
½ teaspoon salt

1 beaten egg
milk (approximately ½ cup)
oil for frying

Put the clams through a meat grinder, add the pepper, and mix with pancake flour, salt, egg and enough milk to make a stiff batter. Drop by small spoonfuls into hot oil and fry until golden brown. Drain on paper towel. Serves 6.

HILDA CROCKETT'S CORN PUDDING

1 cup sugar (½ cup is
 sufficient)
3 tablespoons cornstarch
2 eggs, beaten
1 17-ounce can white cream-
 style corn

1 5⅓-ounce can evaporated
 milk
2 tablespoons butter

In a mixing bowl, combine sugar and cornstarch; add beaten eggs and mix until blended. Pour in the corn and milk and mix thoroughly. Grease a 1½-quart oven-proof casserole and pour in corn mixture. Dot with cubes of butter and bake in a 350-degree oven for approximately 1 hour. Serves 4 to 6.

HILDA CROCKETT'S POUND CAKE

3 sticks butter
3 cups sugar
6 eggs
2 tablespoons lemon extract

1 tablespoon vanilla extract
3 cups flour
1 teaspoon baking powder
1 cup milk

Prepare bundt cake pan by greasing with shortening and dusting with flour. Preheat oven to 350 degrees. In large bowl, cream butter and sugar until light and fluffy. Beat in eggs 2 at a time; continue beating while adding extracts. Sift flour and baking powder together. Reduce speed on mixer; add flour mixture alternately with milk, beginning and ending with flour. Bake for approximately 1 hour or until toothpick comes out clean. Do not overbake. Yields 1 cake.

INDEX

APPETIZERS

Baked Oysters Scarbrough,
  Mount Vernon Inn, 131
Brie in Filo with Pistachio Nut
  Butter, Red Fox Tavern 107
Crab and Spinach Timbale, Inn
  at Little Washington 91
Crab au Four, Le Snail 47
Cucumber Cream Flan,
  Kenmore Inn 136
Frittata Zucchini, Prospect Hill
  75
Ham Swirls, Conyers House 83
Mushrooms Albemarle, Silver
  Thatch Inn 60
Scallop Seviche a la Tallitienne,
  Waterwheel Restaurant 27

BEVERAGES

Hot Spiced Wine, Half Way
  House 171
Piña Colada, Sam Snead's
  Tavern 20
Wine Cooler, Chowning's
  Tavern 176

BREADS

Biscuits, Michie Tavern 51
Blueberry Muffins, Joseph
  Nichols Tavern 12
Pumpkin Muffins, Edinburg
  Mill Restaurant 99
Rich Cream Scones, Kenmore
  Inn 135
Sally Lunn Bread, Gadsby's
  Tavern 123

Sweet Potato Muffins,
  Christiana Campbell's Tavern
  179

DESSERTS

Cakes:

Carrot Cake, Wayside Inn 103
Cheesecake, Milton Warren's
  Ice House 195
Hummingbird Cake,
  Sunnybrook Inn 7
Pound Cake, Hilda Crockett's
  Chesapeake House 200

Ice Creams and Sherbets:

Black Walnut Ice Cream,
  Chowning's Tavern 175
Raspberry Champagne Sorbet,
  Red Fox Tavern 108

Miscellaneous:

Apple Brown Betty, Laurel
  Brigade Inn 116
Apple Cobbler, Michie Tavern
  52
Chocolate Mousse, Miller's 55
Coeur à la Crème with
  Raspberry Sauce, Inn at Little
  Washington 92
Eyemouth Tart, Kenmore Inn
  135
Grand Marnier Creme Torte,
  Bavarian Chef 79
Homemade Colonial Bread
  Pudding, Mount Vernon Inn
  132
Lemon Mousse, Conyers House
  84
Pecan Bars, Williamsburg Inn
  187

Rich Cream Scones, Kenmore
Inn 135
Toffee Shortbread,
McCormick's Pub &
Restaurant 40

Pies:
Buttermilk Pie, Gadsby's
Tavern 124
Chocolate Pecan Pie, Virginian
71
Chocolate Silk Pie, Willson-
Walker House 15
Coconut Raisin Pie, Smithfield
Inn and Tavern 191
German Chocolate Pie, Wharf
Deli & Pub 43
Peanut Butter Pie, Buckhorn Inn
36
Pecan Pie, Ivy Inn 67
Rum Cream Pie, Christiana
Campbell's Tavern 179

Pie Crusts:
Pastry Crust, King's Arms
Tavern 184
Pastry Crust, Miller's 56
Vanilla Wafer Pie Crust, Milton
Warren's Ice House 195

ENTREES
Fowl:
Breast of Chicken Ednam,
Boar's Head Inn 64
Cheddar Chicken, Edinburg
Mill Restaurant 100
Chicken Barbara, Evans Farm
Inn 119

Chicken in Tarragon Cream
Sauce, Waterwheel
Restaurant 28
Chicken Pot Pie, King's Arms
Tavern 183
Chicken Salad, Wharf Deli &
Pub 43
Colonial Fried Chicken, Michie
Tavern 52
Curried Chicken, Laurel
Brigade Inn 115
Duck Breast, Sixty-Seven
Waterloo 88
Roasted Pheasant Stuffed with
Apples, Walnuts and Figs,
Mount Vernon Inn 132
Roast Turkey "Marco Polo,"
Homestead 24
Roast Turkey with Peanut
Dressing, Wayside Inn 104
Turkey Devonshire, Gadsby's
Tavern 124

Meats:
Braised Lamb Shanks, Sky
Chalet Country Inn 96
Fillet Lapin (rabbit), Le Snail 48
Honey Mustard Glazed
Spareribs, Waterwheel
Restaurant 28
Lamb with Raspberry Sauce,
Traveller's Restaurant 167
London Broil, King's Court
Tavern 112
Mandelschnitzel (pork
tenderloin), Bavarian Chef 79
Martha's Delight, Martha
Washington Inn 4

Pecan-Crusted Pork Tenderloin,
Willson-Walker House 16
Prime Rib, Wayside Inn 104
Roast Loin of Pork with Sweet
German Sauerkraut, Sky
Chalet Country Inn 95
Sausage Provencal, La Petite
Auberge 140
Smithfield Ham, Smithfield Inn
and Tavern 192
Stuffed Cabbage Rolls, Joseph
Nichols Tavern 11
Tenderloin of Beef Stuffed with
Oysters, King's Arms Tavern
184
Veal Piccata, Tobacco Company
Restaurant 164
Virginia Ham with Raisin
Sauce, Boar's Head Inn 63

Miscellaneous:
Apple Fritter Pancakes,
Prospect Hill 76
Calzone, Miller's 56
Cheese Omelet, Warm Springs
Inn 31
Fantasio Omelet, Williamsburg
Inn 188
Mexiskins, Sam Snead's Tavern
19
Quesadilla, Portner's 128
Welsh Rarebit, 175

Seafood:
Back Fin Crab Norfolk, La
Petite Auberge 139
Clam Fritters, Hilda Crockett's
Chesapeake House 199
Crab and Spinach Timbale, Inn
at Little Washington 91

Crab au Four, Le Snail 47
Crab Cakes, Hilda Crockett's
Chesapeake House 199
Crab Imperial, Sam Miller's
Warehouse 159
Crab Imperial, Traveller's
Restaurant 168
Crab Soup, Sam Miller's
Warehouse 160
Flounder Fillet, Martha
Washington Inn 3
Jambalaya, McCormick's Pub &
Restaurant 39
Jambalaya, Miller's 55
Mountain Trout, Conyers
House 84
Oysters a la Jefferson, Lemaire
Restaurant 156
Scallop and Shrimp Casserole,
Ivy Inn 67
Seafood Neptune, Milton
Warren's Ice House 195
Shrimp and Lobster, A Made
Dish of, Christiana
Campbell's Tavern 180
Shrimp Salad, Hanover Tavern
147
Shrimp Scampi, Milton
Warren's Ice House 196
Soft-Shelled Crabs, La Petite
Auberge 139

SALADS
Avocado Mousse, Laurel
Brigade Inn 116
Broccoli Salad, Buckhorn Inn 35
Chicken Salad, Wharf Deli &
Pub 43
Christmas Cranberry Salad,
Sunnybrook Inn 8

Pasta Light-Line Salad, Tobacco
Company Restaurant 163
Salad and Dressing, Joseph
Nichols Tavern 12
Shrimp Salad, Hanover Tavern
147
Strawberry Salad, Portner's 127

SANDWICHES
Welsh Rarebit, Chowning's
Tavern 175

SAUCES, STOCKS, GRAVIES AND DRESSINGS
Blue Cheese Dressing, Fox
Head Inn 152
Bordelaise Sauce, King's Court
Tavern 112
Crock Pot Apple Butter, Warm
Springs Inn, 32
Demi-glace, Tobacco Company
Restaurant 164
Dressing, Joseph Nichols
Tavern 12
Feta, Basil, Shrimp & Tomato
Sauce, Virginian 71
French Dressing, Half Way
House 172
Hard Sauce, Laurel Brigade Inn
116
House Dressing, Sam Snead's
Tavern 19
Mint Sauce, Silver Thatch Inn
60
Mornay Sauce, Homestead 24
Peach Butter, Warm Springs Inn
31
Peanut Dressing, Wayside Inn
104

Raisin Sauce, Boar's Head Inn
63
Raspberry Poppy Seed
Dressing, Homestead 23
Red Eye Gravy, Martha
Washington Inn 4
Salsa Cilentro, Portner's 128
Sausage Gravy, Edinburg Mill
Restaurant 99
Veal Stock, Sixty-Seven
Waterloo 88

SOUPS
Acorn Squash Bisque,
Sixty-Seven Waterloo 87
Black Bean Soup with
Smithfield Ham and Sherry,
Lemaire Restaurant 155
Broccoli and Cheese Soup,
Wharf Deli & Pub 44
Caldo Gallego (bean soup),
Virginian 72
Champagne Melon Soup, Ivy
Inn 68
Cream of Watercress,
Homestead 23
Hungarian Goulash Soup,
Bavarian Chef 80
Potato Soup, King's Court
Tavern 111

VEGETABLES AND FRUITS
Asparagus and Pea Casserole,
Evans Farm Inn 120
Bourbon Sweet Potatoes, Olde
Mudd Tavern 143
Cheese Corn, Hanover Tavern
148

Corn Pudding, Hilda Crockett's
Chesapeake House 200
Creamed Spinach, Olde Mudd
Tavern 144
Cymling Cakes, Fox Head
Inn 151
Frittata Zucchini, Prospect
Hill 75
Green Beans, Half Way
House 171
Marinated Carrots, Buckhorn
Inn 36
Mexiskins, Sam Snead's Tavern
19
Spaghetti Squash, Silver Thatch
Inn 59

Stewed Apples, Hanover
Tavern 147
Stewed Tomatoes, Michie
Tavern 51
Stewed Tomatoes, Smithfield
Inn and Tavern 191
Stuffed Cabbage Rolls, Joseph
Nichols Tavern 11
Three-Vegetable Casserole,
Sunnybrook Inn 8
Zucchini in Tomato Sauce, Old
Mudd Tavern 143

Library of Congress Cataloging in Publication Data

O'Brien, Dawn.
  Virginia's historic restaurants and their recipes.

  Includes index.
  1. Cookery, American—Virginia.   2. Restaurants,
lunch rooms, etc.—Virginia.   3. Historic buildings—
Virginia.   I. Title.
TX715.0'29   1984   641.5'09755   84-2801
ISBN 0-89587-068-1